Live Well
Eat Well

For Hilkey

Janie Ebenger

Janie Ebinger

Live Well
Eat Well

JANIE'S TWIST ON SALADS, SANDWICHES, AND WRAPS

MOUNTAIN ARBOR
PRESS

MOUNTAIN ARBOR
PRESS
Alpharetta, GA

Dedication

I am dedicating this book, *Live Well, Eat Well: Janie's Twist on Salads, Sandwiches, & Wraps*, to all the children of the world. They do not ask to be born. They do not ask to be abused. My wish is that no child ever again will go to sleep hungry or afraid; die from the lack of food to eat, clean water to drink, or medication for diseases; or suffer abuse and neglect. Our children, grandchildren and great-grandchildren either born to us, adopted, fostered, through friendship or through marriage are a gift from God and should be raised with love, care, and nurturing the way God intended.

I wish to continue to give thanks to God, our Lord and Savior, for allowing me to further pursue my creativity by giving me the courage and strength to write my third book *Live Well, Eat Well: Janie's Twist on Salads, Sandwiches, & Wraps*.

On June 8, 2012 my dear friend Shawn W. Fortier left this life to join our Father in heaven. I, your loving family, & multitude of friends will forever miss you. Rest in peace Shawn, rest in peace. Until we meet again in a better place.

Contents

Introduction

I am and have been for many years a chef at Sycamore Hills Golf Club in Fort Wayne, Indiana. Your journey continues through my world of simply wonderful recipes. This adventure takes us on a trip through buffet salads, more entrée salads, some sandwiches & wraps. My twist is that they can be made into each other, in other words they are all one in the same. I want everyone to remember that anything you use to make a great salad can be used on a bread or tortilla of some sort to make a great sandwich or wrap, anything you can put on bread or in a tortilla to make a great sandwich or wrap can be put with lettuces, spinach, cabbages, or arugula to make a great salad. But…there are exceptions to everything.

Some of the salads even in my wildest dreams I would not attempt to make into a sandwich or wrap; some of the sandwiches or wraps in my wildest dreams I would not make into a salad, but that does not mean you cannot. In the sandwich and wrap selections, I have given the directions to make a salad out of them. I have not given the directions on how to make sandwiches out of the buffet and entrée salads. Just pick your bread or tortilla, then go for it. All the buffet salad recipes have no quantities for them. That is because how much you make depends on how much you need. All the entrée salad recipes are for two servings as well as the sandwich and wrap recipes.

You will notice that all the recipe names start with a person. That is because I have named them all after family and friends. This is because they are all special to me.

What is a buffet salad? My definition is unofficial, but here it is anyway: Any combination of fruits, vegetables, poultry, beef, pork, fish, seafood, cheese, vinaigrettes, mayonnaise dressings, herbs, spices, garlic, nuts, grains, pastas, and beans—well you get the idea. Some people refer to them as composed salads. The recipes are endless. These salads are the first recipes in this book—the ones with no quantities in the ingredients. Buffet salads can be made of as few as three different ingredients or as many as ten or more. Buffet salads are a great way to use leftovers.

Those bakers that were last night's hot potatoes can be tonight's potato salad along with the rest of the grilled steak. It is called "Steak and Potato Salad" made with Dijon vinaigrette accompanied with a dinner salad and crusty bread. What a nice dinner for a hot summer night. Even the kids like it. Most of these buffet salads will last five days in the fridge. Some of them can be made two to three days ahead of time. Some should be mixed the day they are used, especially the ones with citrus or pineapple with chicken, fish, or seafood, because the acid in the citrus or pineapple breaks down the protein in the chicken making it mushy. The ones made with fish or seafood using citrus or pineapple can make them tuff or chewy because of the chemical reaction from the acids in the citrus or pineapple. Salads made with a mayonnaise-based dressing, even if it has citrus juice or pineapple, will not have this effect as fast because of the mayonnaise. It neutralizes the acids slowing down the breakdown of the proteins, giving you one more day.

Growing up I never knew the term buffet salad. All I knew was potato salad, macaroni salad (my favorite even now), and coleslaw. There was one way to make them—my mom made the best. I learned really quickly that there is no right or wrong way to make a particular buffet salad. Add your own personal ideas. I now have probably fifteen to twenty different recipes at least for slaws, even more for macaroni salads and potato salads. I have lost count. Change one ingredient you have made a whole new salad. I was amazed when I started cooking professionally as an adult. Once I started making vinaigrettes and buffet salads at the hotels, clubs, and restaurants I worked at, I could not learn enough. They are such fun to create, the different flavors, textures and colors will simply amaze you, your family and guests.

Some of the vinaigrettes in this book are found in my *Simply Vinaigrettes from Ancho Chili to White Wine* or *Janie's Simply Entrée Salads for Two* cookbooks. You do not have to own these books to use this one. I have given you the recipe for each vinaigrette or dressing that I use in this book, even though it may be in one of my others. I will also specify if a vinaigrette or dressing is in one of my other books. I will have *Simply Vinaigrettes* or *Janie's Simply Entrée* in the ingredients list (the quantities will be smaller than what is in the "*Simply Vinaigrettes*" recipe book). My suggestion for a dressing or vinaigrette for each recipe is just that—a suggestion. I offer you the choice of using your own recipes, buying premade products at the store, or making fresh vinaigrettes and dressings for your salad. As I always say fresh is best.

The salads that are made with only oil (no vinegar) can be made with canola, salad, vegetable, or extra virgin olive oils, whichever you prefer. Some are made with both; the choice is yours. There is an oil blend that you can purchase; it is a blend of canola and extra virgin olive oil—eighty percent canola and twenty percent extra virgin olive oil. You can purchase canola, salad, vegetable oils and extra virgin olive oil separate to blend your own. Some of the salads are best when made with canola, salad, or vegetable oil, and others are best when made with extra virgin olive oil.

If there is a specialty store in your area that sells balsamic vinegars that are infused with flavors and extra virgin olive oils infused with flavors, I encourage you to use them. I am fortunate to have *The Olive Twist* near me with two locations: Auburn, Indiana & Fort Wayne, Indiana. Both of these cities are in northeast Indiana. There is another store of this kind in Granger, Indiana called *The Olive Branch*.

Another word about vinaigrettes: they can be made fat free simply by replacing the oils with fruit juice, frozen, bottled, or fresh; vegetable juices, bottled or fresh; and even vegetable stock. Never use water; that only deletes the taste. They can also be made sugar free by using sugar or honey substitutes or leaving the sugar or honey out. I blend all my vinaigrettes with a hand held blender or electric blender.

When it comes to the herbs, I use fresh, frozen, ground, or dried. Some salads are just not right with dried herbs; for some, it does not matter. I have not found frozen herbs in a small amount. The only way I have seen them available frozen is in ten pound boxes. If you want to purchase large quantities of fresh herbs, I suggest that the fresh herbs be chopped then placed in the zipper lock bags in smaller amounts then frozen. Dried herbs can be bought in large quantities then frozen to keep them longer. Fresh herbs can also be placed on a cookie sheet, dried overnight in a 250 degree oven, or left out in a dry warm place away from heat or sunlight to dry then stored in closed containers. Dried herbs should not be kept on the shelf for longer than six months. They lose flavor and nutritional value. If you store them in the freezer, you can get a few more months of use out of them.

There is a variety of vegetarian style salads and sandwiches included in this book. Any variety of meats, poultry, fish, seafood, pork, or beef can be added to them, even processed meats such as salamis, pepperoni, sausages and lunch meats. You are not limited to the cheeses you use. If you do not like cheddar, use swiss. If you do not like shredded cheese, then dice it or leave it out. You can also replace it with a vegetable or fruit you like.

Nuts! There are so many different varieties—cashews, walnuts, peanuts (these are actually a legume; they grow underground), pecans, almonds, black walnuts, filbert nuts, pine nuts (all these are also known as tree nuts), and many more. It is the same with seeds—sesame seeds (white or black), sunflower seeds, pumpkin seeds, quinoa seeds (they are the small, white, round seeds found in bird feed; they are great toasted and are gluten free), and watermelon. Seeds are great especially when toasted. I could go on and on about the varieties of nuts and seeds.

There are at least one hundred types of pastas and grains! Have you ever tried wheat berries? They're unbelievable! I recommend tabbuleah (cracked bulgur wheat) couscous and barley just to mention a few. How about wild rice or jasmine rice? Both are fantastic. Don't forget beans! Do not be afraid; they are your friends. They can be dried or canned. If you use canned, rinse them well. There are pinto beans, black beans, kidney beans, anastasia beans, great northerners, calypso beans, plus many more.

What about fruits? They come canned, dried, frozen, or fresh, not to mention the varieties of some of them. There are many types of apples, oranges and grapes just to mention some. Vegetables! Where do I begin? Onions, tomatoes (they are actually a fruit). Do not forget tomatillos (they look like a small, green tomato and are delicious with a crisp tart taste). There is also jicama, chayote squash, and potatoes. I cannot begin to count the varieties. Do not be afraid to use more than one variety of potato in a salad. Squashes and root vegetables (celery root, carrots, parsnips, beets, calarabi, turnips, and many more) are also great.

Remember to use fresh grown fruits and vegetables whenever possible.

There are no quantities given in these recipes for the buffet salads, (the entrée salads are for two servings, but they can be easily increased for more servings), because the quantities depend on how much you need to make. All the buffet salads in this recipe book can be used as entrée salads and all the entree salads can be used for buffet salads. If you know there will be fifty hungry people eating your buffet salads, then use five pounds of pasta. That is before it is cooked weight; rice will double in volume, and meats shrink. If you are going to make a salad that uses chicken as the main ingredient, start with ten pounds of raw meat for fifty people, especially if it has bones in it.

Never drown a salad in the vinaigrette or dressing. Only use what is needed to make it flavorful and moist. Vinaigrettes make great additions to any sandwich—either put on the bread or dipped into it. Now, I would bet you are asking, "Why does she use the terms vinaigrettes and dressings? Are they not the same?" Not to me. A vinaigrette is made with vinegar, juices or stocks of some sort, and oils (or if I am making them fat free, I use juice or vegetable stock; I never add water because it only dilutes the flavor). A dressing is a mayonnaise-based product. This is not an official ruling. It is only my personal opinion. I do have some dressings that are made with mayonnaise, vinegar, and oils. That is because I use mayonnaise instead of raw egg to make creamy vinaigrettes. This can be done to any vinaigrette if you prefer them creamy; just blend in some mayonnaise until it is the texture and color you want, but be careful, because too much mayonnaise will make it taste like flavored mayonnaise. The difference between salad dressing and mayonnaise is that salad dressing has more lemon juice and sugar, so it is tarter and sweeter. It also has no egg yolks. There are some recipes that have a vinaigrette or dressing that you cannot find in a store. I have given you the recipe and the quantities to make the recipe. If you do not use it all in the salad, just keep it in a covered container in the fridge. Vinaigrettes will keep for months, but mayonnaise dressings keep for two weeks only.

A small amount of xanthan gum can be added to any vinaigrette to thicken it slightly. I do not like thin watery vinaigrettes, I want it to stick to the food it is used on. I learned about xanthan gum after I wrote my other two recipe books. It can be bought at any food store, even the large chains; it is usually with the gluten free foods. A little goes a long way—for a recipe making six cups of vinaigrette a 1/4 to a 1/2 teaspoon should work nicely. You can always add more. If you add too much, you must increase the other ingredients, making much more than you want. I know I have.

I have recipes for entrée salads in this book. I do not go on about them in this introduction because I did that in detail in my recipe book *Janie's Simply Entrée Salads for Two.* You will notice that I keep referring you to other recipes for directions on how to toast nuts, dry fruit, peel fruit, make candied nuts, etc. this is because it is silly for me to keep giving these directions, and what better way to get you to read all the recipes.

I hope you enjoy this book as much as I did writing it for you. Always make sure you read the recipe all the way through before starting to avoid any surprises. There is nothing worse than starting a recipe only to find out you do not have something you need or finding you do not like something so you have to go to the store again.

The abbreviations I use for the ingredients and measurements are as follows:

c.-cup
t.-teaspoon
T.-tablespoon
oz.-ounce
lbs.-pounds
evoo.-extra virgin olive oil
fgbp.-fresh ground black pepper
cbp.-cracked black pepper
ks.-kosher salt
hrs.- hours
min.-minute
bnch. bunch

All the measurements for garlic, shallots, herbs, onions, and nuts are after they have been chopped, ground or pureed.

Let the journey continue, enjoy the adventure. Remember: *Live Well, Eat Well.*

Orville Cucumbers, Tomatoes, Red Onion in Sweet & Sour Basil Vinaigrette

Cucumbers
Roma or salad tomatoes
Red onion
Sweet and sour basil vinaigrette (Simply Vinaigrettes)
Ks.
Fgbp.

Sweet and sour! Along with fresh cucumbers, tomatoes, and red onion, the first bite will steal your taste buds' hearts. When you decide to prepare this salad, the first thing to do is decide if you are going to use regular cucumbers or English cucumbers (or burp less as they are sometimes called). If you use regular cucumbers, they can be peeled or unpeeled with the seeds removed or left in. Using regular cucumbers in this salad is much nicer if you cut the cucumbers in 4 pieces the long way, and then cut them into bite size pieces. When I use English cucumbers I leave them whole and unpeeled. Slice them into thin slices about 1/8 inch thick. English cucumbers can also be cut in four pieces the long way and then cut into bite size pieces. After deciding what cucumbers to use, then move on to the tomatoes. I prefer to use Roma tomatoes. They are meatier, taste better, and the color is usually a deeper red. I have made this salad using green tomatoes, and the result was delicious. If they are fresh grown, they are even better. When using roma tomatoes, cut off the stem end. Cut into quarters, remove the seeds, then cut each quarter into 2 pieces. If you use salad tomatoes, remove the core, cut in half, then remove the seeds. I always remove the seeds; it is just nicer that way. If you do not care for red onion, then use a white, sweet onion. Peel the onion, cut into bite size pieces.

Carefully toss the cucumbers, tomatoes, and onions together with the sweet & sour basil vinaigrette adding the salt (a small amount of salt, it takes the water out of the cucumbers, making the salad watery) and pepper. I always use kosher salt; the flavor is better and less is used. Of course, sea salt is also an excellent choice. When it comes to pepper, I only use fresh ground white, black, or a blend of different peppercorns. This salad is best when it is made 2 to 3 days ahead of time so it can marinade. Another way I like to serve this salad is to either toss it with baby greens, fresh spinach, arugula, or a mix of all 3. Put it in a serving bowl for all to enjoy or place the lettuce choice on a large serving platter then top with the salad mix. Fresh shaved or grated parmesan or Romano cheese on top is very delicious. Chicken marinated in the sweet & sour basil vinaigrette then grilled (if you marinade a chicken in a vinaigrette that contains a large amount of sugar or honey as the sweet & sour basil does, watch it carefully as it grills because the sugar or honey will burn easily) can also be added. Of course fish, pork, seafood, or beef can also be added.

Sweet & Sour Basil Vinaigrette

1 T. fresh basil
1 T. fresh garlic
1 c. apple cider vinegar
1 c. evoo
1 c. canola or salad oil
1 c. sugar or sugar substitute
1 t. ks.
1 1/2 t. fgbp

Add all the ingredients together blend well. From my experience, all vinaigrettes will keep for months if kept in a closed container in the fridge and only get better with time.

Helen Bleu Cheese Potato Salad in Bleu Cheese Vinaigrette

Potatoes (Yukon gold, red skin, fingerling, bakers, purple just to mention a few types)
Green onions or chives
Bleu cheese crumbles
Bleu cheese vinaigrette (Simply Vinaigrettes)
Ks.
Fgbp.

There is not a potato that would not be proud to be in this salad. When you choose a potato for your salad there are no limits. This is a great way to use leftover baked or roasted potatoes. I like to leave the skin on when making potato salad. Remember you can use several different types of potatoes in the salad. Wash them well, then dice or leave them whole. Place potatoes in cold water in a large pot, cook until done. Test the potatoes with a knife or fork for doneness. Do not overcook them because mushy potatoes are not good for potato salad unless you are making smashed potato salad. Drain the potatoes well. Putting them in ice water to chill works great; let cool completely if they are still warm. Otherwise, when you add the bleu cheese crumbles, they will melt slightly. The result will be a gloppy mess. Dice them if you didn't before cooking; you can also slice or crumble them with your hands. Slice the green onions or chives, add them to the potatoes. Add the bleu cheese crumbles and the salt (go easy with the salt; there's plenty in the bleu cheese) and pepper (cracked black pepper is even better in this salad). Then add the bleu cheese vinaigrette, tossing well to coat all the potatoes. The vinaigrette will soak into the potatoes. It may be necessary to add more before serving. This salad, as with most of my buffet salads, is best when made 2 to 3 days ahead chilled well before serving. This salad goes great with burgers, dogs, ribs, and steaks or actually any grilled or barbequed foods you like. Cooked meats or chicken can be added to this salad along with some bell peppers or other vegetables to make a complete meal.

Bleu Cheese Vinaigrette

2 c. bleu cheese crumbles
1 c. evoo
1 c. canola or salad oil
1 c. apple cider vinegar
1 T. cbp
1 T. dried basil
1 T. chopped garlic
1/2 t. ks (optional)

I prefer my bleu cheese vinaigrette chunky. To do this blend all the ingredients together except the bleu cheese with a hand blender. I add the bleu cheese, mixing it in with a spoon or wire whisk. If you like it creamy, blend with all the ingredients to start with. I like to add some heat to this vinaigrette when the occasion calls for it (which means every time for me). The heat you use is up to you—jalapenos, habañeros, cayenne pepper, crushed red chilies, or even ghost chilies.

Charles Sweet Marinated Vegetable

Zucchini squash
Yellow squash
Red onion
Red bell peppers
Yellow bell peppers
Jicama
Mushrooms (button, shitake, crimini, or Portobello to
    mention a few)
Carrots (orange, red or yellow regular size or baby)
Sweet Italian Vinaigrette (Janie's Simply Entrée)
Ks.
Fgbp.

Friends called and invited you to a cookout at their home on Saturday, and asked you to bring a salad that will go great with whatever is grilled. You respond with "I have the perfect salad and vinaigrette for it." This vinaigrette is excellent to marinate grilled meats. It is Wednesday you tell them you will bring some marinade by on Friday so they can marinate the meats, but you will make the salad today so it can be well marinated by Saturday. You, your salad, and your marinade are the hit of the party. This is such an easy simple salad to make. There are a lot of vegetables that can be used instead or with the ones I have selected. The zucchini and yellow squash can be sliced or diced with the seeds left in. I do not peel them. The choice is yours. The red onion is peeled cut into bite size pieces if you do not like red onion then use a sweet white variety. Small pearl or cocktail onions as they are sometimes called work well also as does green onion. The bell peppers are cut into bite size pieces or julienne cut (cut into thin strips). The jicama is peeled much like an apple then diced into bite size pieces. What is a jicama you ask? It is a vegetable that comes from Mexico and South America. It is a bulbous root vegetable with a thin brown skin and white crunchy flesh. It has a sweet nutty flavor that is good raw or cooked. Jicama easily takes on the flavors of what it is used with. Mushrooms let's talk mushrooms. Whatever variety you choose just remove the stems slice or dice (do not throw the stems away; use for soups or sauces.) Carrots! Well let's see there are standard orange, red, and yellow, regular size and shape or baby. I prefer the standard carrot size and shape, simply peel slice very thin they remain crisp when put with vinaigrettes. As you prepare all the vegetables for this salad put them in a large mixing bowl together toss with the sweet Italian vinaigrette add salt and pepper refrigerate to get cold. For the best flavor make at least 3 days before use. This salad, as with most of my recipes, can be kicked up a notch with the addition of some heat. The choice is yours.

Sweet Italian Vinaigrette

1 1/2 c. sugar or artificial sweetener
3 c. evoo
3 c. canola or salad oil
3 T. Italian seasoning
1/2 t. ks
1 t. fgbp

Sweet! Yes sweet! And Italian to boot! This vinaigrette is easy, fast and tasty to make. Put everything together in a mixing bowl use a spoon or wire whip blending well. The sweet herby taste only gets better the longer it sits in the fridge. Try using this on grilled or sautéed vegetables. Just think what it will do for a pasta salad with Italian meats, roasted vegetables and shaved parmesan cheese. I have made this vinaigrette with sugar and artificial sweeteners both are great.

Linda M. Pasta Salad Tossed in Sweet Tomato Vinaigrette

Pasta (any variety)
Red bell peppers (roasted)
Yellow bell peppers (roasted)
Green onion
Artichoke hearts
Shredded parmesan cheese
Sweet Tomato vinaigrette (Simply Vinaigrettes)
Ks.
Fgbp.

If you have never tasted a pasta salad made with a sweet vinaigrette, you must try this one. There are over one hundred types of pasta available. If you have a pasta maker, you can really have some fun. Some people like their pasta cooked al dente (what I call half-done, which is fine if the pasta is going to be cooked again say in a baked pasta dish). I do not for pasta salad; I want it done. The roasted bell peppers can be bought in the store already roasted (do not throw away the liquid the roasted bell peppers are packed in it is full of flavor for soups and sauces), or you can roast them in the oven. Preheat the oven to 350 degrees, coat the bell peppers with evoo or canola oil, place them on a cookie sheet, put it in preheated oven, and check every 10 minutes. Turn the peppers when they start to brown. When the skin blisters they are done. Carefully remove from oven and place in a bowl cover with plastic wrap or put in a paper sack close tightly, let them sct for at least 30 minutes. Carefully remove from the bowl or bag. The center is full of liquid and is very hot. Carefully pull them apart, remove seeds and membranes, and peel off the skin. Do not rinse in water; that removes a lot of the flavor. If you can cook them even a day ahead, let sit in the fridge until you're ready to use them. That is even safer. Dice or julienne cut the bell peppers. The green onions can be cut into strings or sliced. Artichoke hearts can be bought at most grocery stores in cans or jars; just drain them. Artichoke hearts can be left whole or cut into quarters or halves. I prefer to shred my own parmesan cheese, but buying it already shredded is okay. To make this delicious treat simply toss everything together with the sweet tomato vinaigrette. Add the salt and pepper. To make this salad more of a whole meal, try adding sliced, diced, or julienne salami, pepperoni, chicken, beef, pork, or shrimp. Black and or green olives are nice also added. Pasta salad is also great made with the sweet Italian vinaigrette in the recipe for Charles Sweet Marinated Vegetable.

Sweet Tomato Vinaigrette

1/2 c. sweet onion (red, white or yellow)
1/2 c. sugar or sugar substitute
3 c. diced tomato packed in water
1 T. dried thyme
1 T. dried basil
1 c. apple cider vinegar
2 c. canola or salad oil
1/2 t. ks
1 t. fgbp

Canned tomatoes? Really canned tomatoes? Yes! You can use fresh diced if you prefer, but there is just something about the taste and texture of canned tomatoes that just works well. Drain them very well, save the tomato juice for soups or to drink. Place the well-drained tomatoes in a mixing bowl dice the tomatoes smaller if the pieces are too large for your taste. I prefer small diced. Add the rest of the ingredients mix well with a spoon. If you use a hand blender, you will have tomato juice. To get the full effect of the flavors of this vinaigrette let sit in the fridge for a week before using.

Kay Southwest Black Bean, Jicama & Roast Corn

Roasted corn
Black beans
Jicama
Red bell peppers
Red onion
Garlic
Cilantro vinaigrette (Simply Vinaigrettes)
Ks.
Fgbp.

Roasting sweet corn on the cob is the real secret to this salad's flavor. I take ears of sweet corn, pull down the husks, and remove the silk. I then coat the ears with oil and pull the husks back up over the corn. If you have a grill, it is perfect for roasting the corn. Lay the ears on the grill over hot coals turning often so the corn does not burn. If you do not have a grill or do not want to roast it that way then put it in the oven preheated to 350 degrees roast for thirty minutes. If you do not want to use roasting ears then use frozen corn kernels. Toss in a small amount of oil place on a cookie sheet in the oven for 10 minutes. Be careful because if you leave it in the oven to long it will dry out or burn. If you roast ears let cool until you can safely handle remove the husks cut the kernels off the cobs into a mixing bowl.

The black beans can be bought canned already cooked or dry that you cook yourself. If you cook them yourself add garlic and onions to the water for flavor. Jalapenos can also be added for flavor when cooking. Whether you use canned or dry, always rinse them well under cold running water to rinse off the starch. If you do not, the rest of the ingredients will change color and loose flavor. After you have decided to use canned or dry black beans or roasting ears, you can start preparing this wonderful salad. After you have prepared the beans and corn, let them cool, then combine in a bowl. Cut the red bell peppers in half, remove the seeds and membranes, dice small, and add to beans and corn. Peel the jicama, and either dice or julienne cut them. Add to beans and corn. Peel, dice or julienne cut the red onion, and add to the rest of mix. Add the fresh chopped garlic, salt, and pepper. This salad really needs salt and pepper. Toss everything together with the cilantro vinaigrette, being careful not to smash the black beans. By the way, if you can your own corn, it can be used also.

Cilantro Vinaigrette

2 c. fresh cilantro
1 T. fresh garlic
1 T. dijon mustard
2 c. evoo
2 c. canola or salad oil
2 c. apple cider vinegar
1 t. ks
1 1/2 t. fgbp

Yes dried cilantro can be used. Fresh cilantro is usually grown in sandy soil so rinse well, shake off water, and blot dry if necessary. Remove from stems, and discard them or save to add to soups or stocks. It is not necessary to chop the garlic; it will be blended with either a hand blender or electric blender. Add the rest of the ingredients and blend well.

Paul H. Parpadelli Pasta with Chicken in Smoked Tomato Vinaigrette

Parpadelli pasta
Chicken (white or dark meat baked, grilled, roasted or boiled)
Red bell peppers
Yellow bell peppers
Red onion
Smoked Tomato vinaigrette (recipe follows)
Ks.
Fgbp.

Parpadelli pasta? What in the world is that? Remember there are over 100 types of pasta and new shapes made every day. Parpadelli pasta is long, wide, and fairly thick with black pepper in it. Delicious! Delicious! To cook this pasta, boil a large amount of salted water, (salt is added to the water to make the water get hotter, not to flavor the pasta) and add the pasta. Cook until it is done then place in ice water to stop the cooking to chill it fast. Drain well, and toss with a small amount of oil so the pasta does not stick together. The chicken can be leftover. Just shred or dice and add to pasta. If you like marinated chicken, then marinate it in some in the smoked tomato vinaigrette before cooking. To prepare the bell peppers, simply remove the stems, seeds, and membranes, then dice or julienne cut and add to pasta and chicken. Peel, dice or julienne cut the red onion and add to the rest. Add salt and pepper toss well with the smoked tomato vinaigrette.

Smoked Tomato Vinaigrette (Simple, Fast, and Easy Version)

3 c. canned tomatoes (packed in water or juice)
liquid smoke to taste (a little goes a long way)
1 c. cider vinegar
1 c. evoo
1 c. canola or salad oil
1 t. garlic
1 t. dried thyme
1/2 t. ks
1 t. fgbp

Drain the tomatoes the liquid can be saved for soup or sauces. Place them in a blender add the rest of the ingredients blend well. The tomatoes can also be chopped well with a knife, or you can use a hand held blender. To smoke tomatoes, there are two easy ways I recommend. The first is to start a wood or charcoal fire in the grill. When the coals or wood are really hot, cut the tomatoes in half, remove the seeds, and place on the grill so the juice drips on the coals. Close the cover and let smoke for 5 minutes. Be very careful when removing the tomatoes they become very soft. Let them sit and cool, then carefully remove the skin, then blend with the rest of the ingredients. The second way is using a cake pan with a wire rack or an indoor smoker. Place wood chips in water to soak; if you do not soak the wood chips first a fire will start. Remove the wood chips from the water and place in the pan or smoker. Place the rack over the wood, and place the tomatoes on the rack. Place the container over the flame on the stove. When the wood gets hot and starts to smoke, wait 10 minutes then check to see if the tomatoes are smoked enough. Let cool peel then blend with the rest of the ingredients.

Christopher T. Asian Cabbage with Seafood in Dill Dijon Vinaigrette

Cabbage (green, nappa or red)
Crab meat (imitation or real)
Baby shrimp
Cilantro
Sesame oil
Dill Dijon vinaigrette (recipe follows)

Cabbage is not just for coleslaw anymore. Coleslaw does not have to be made with only green cabbage. Nappa cabbage, or Chinese cabbage as it is also called, is much sweeter and lighter. It has the look of lace. If you use all 3 varieties I have mentioned you will have a beautiful salad with a variety of textures. To prepare this salad, start by slicing the cabbages very thin. Mix it all together then either shred or chop the crab meat. The baby shrimp can be found in the frozen food section of the grocery. It will thaw in cold water very fast or overnight in the fridge. Frozen shrimp contains a lot of water it needs to be removed. To do this place the thawed shrimp in a dish towel or paper towel wrap squeeze out the excess water. Add the crab meat and shrimp together and mix well. This will ensure even distribution of both in the salad. Pull the cilantro leaves off the stems, chop fine, and then combine with the cabbages, crabmeat, and shrimp. Toss well, then add some sesame oil, but be careful not to add too much. It can overpower the other tastes. Add the dill dijon vinaigrette mix well let marinade for 2 or 3 days before eating. Sesame oil can also be added to the dill dijon vinaigrette instead of putting in the salad. Crushed red chilies can be added for extra taste. This salad is very good on fish sandwiches or served with a barbeque dinner.

Dill Dijon Vinaigrette

1 c. dijon mustard
1/4 c. dill (fresh, dried or frozen)
2 c. cider vinegar
2 c. canola or salad oil
2 c. evoo
1/2 t. ks
1 t. fgbp
1 T. garlic
1/2 t. crushed red chilies (optional)

Blend all the ingredients together well.

Samantha Yukon Gold Dill Dijon Potato Salad

Yukon gold potatoes
Green onions
Ks.
Fgbp.
Dill Dijon vinaigrette (recipe given in the recipe for Asian Cabbage with Seafood)

You have never heard of Yukon gold potatoes, and why 2 salads with dill Dijon vinaigrette? Well you are in for an experience! I use the dill dijon vinaigrette for both these salads because it really works. Yukon gold potatoes are naturally sweet. Roasting them really brings it out. They are good boiled also but roasting is the best way. This salad is so easy to make you want to toss it before the potatoes get cold. Why you ask? Because the dill dijon vinaigrette soaks right into the hot potatoes. To make this salad, start by washing the potatoes in cold water while the oven is heating to 350-400 degrees. After washing, cut into bite size pieces or leave whole, (they will be very hot to cut after cooking). If you roast whole smash with a potato masher just to break up. Toss in evoo with kosher salt and black pepper, put in a roasting pan, and place in preheated oven for 30 to 40 minutes. After the potatoes are done, remove from oven let sit 5 minutes for starch to set.

While the potatoes are cooking slice the green onions, if you have not made the vinaigrette now is the time. Dump the potatoes into a mixing bowl add onions, vinaigrette, salt and pepper toss well to coat all the potatoes be careful they are very hot. This salad needs to sit in the fridge for 2 to 3 days before using for the best flavor. Chicken or beef can be added to this salad for a complete meal along with a dinner salad. Fresh arugula is another option to add flavor & texture. If you love cheese with potato salad try adding some bleu cheese, shredded cheddar or dill Havarti. Do not add the cheese until the potato salad is well chilled. It will glob if you do not. Heat for extra kick can be added also.

Dee Brussels Sprouts Marinated in Tarragon Vinaigrette

Brussels Sprouts (fresh or frozen)
Carrots (orange, yellow or red)
Tarragon vinaigrette (recipe follows) ks.
Fgbp.

Brussels sprouts are not just for steaming and serving with butter or hollandaise sauce. They are absolutely wonderful when chilled with a vinaigrette. Tarragon is such a good flavorful, fragrant herb. I can smell it now. I start by boiling water with salt add the sprouts let come to boil again cook for 5 minutes for frozen 8 minutes for fresh. Cook until fork tender drain well put in a bowl add the tarragon vinaigrette while still hot. The vinaigrette soaks in fast cooling them down so the carrots can be added. Shred, slice, dice, or julienne the carrots, run under cold water to rinse so your salad won't turn orange from the carrots. Make sure you add the salt and pepper; this salad needs it. If you do not like tarragon, there are several different vinaigrettes that are great with Brussels sprouts. There are lots of other choices in this book. Pork, chicken, beef, seafood, or fish can be added to this salad.

Tarragon Vinaigrette

2 c. tarragon vinegar
1/4 c. dried tarragon
1 T. garlic
1 T. Dijon mustard
2 c. canola or salad oil
2 c. evoo
1 t. ks
1 1/2 t. fgbp

What if I cannot find tarragon vinegar? Use cider or rice wine vinegar instead. Add all the ingredients together and blend well. If you do not use all the vinaigrette, store in a closed container in the fridge; it will last for months.

Billy Pecan Pesto Marinated Vegetables

Pecan Pesto (recipe follows)
Zucchini squash
Yellow squash
Cauliflower
Broccoli
Red onion
Asparagus tips
Mushrooms (any varieties)

Have you had your vegetables today? This is a great way to get them. Hubbies and kids like this salad also. The crunch and flavors of these vegetables is just amazing. Keep them raw it will not work if they are cooked. When the pecan pesto is made with fresh basil it is simply amazing. Start preparing the vegetables by slicing them all very thin (thin is the trick they keep their crunch). On the asparagus, only use about the first 3 inches. Save the rest for soup. There are a lot more vegetables that are great for this salad such as chayote, rutabaga, turnips, and tomatoes just to mention a few. I do not add salt to this vegetable mix it is in the pesto recipe black pepper can be added now and in the pesto.

Pecan Pesto

pecans
fresh basil
garlic
parmesan cheese (shredded)
evoo
Fgbp.
Ks.

Pesto? What is a Pesto? The word Pesto in Italian means "pounded." It is a combination of fresh basil, pine nuts, garlic, parmesan cheese, or pecorino cheese. I do not like pine nuts so I choose to use pecans. It can be made using a mortar and pestle, blender or food processor. I give no quantities because the flavor depends on how much garlic you want. Everything should be tasted in each bite. The garlic should not be a sharp bite on the tongue; rather an "oh, okay, there you are garlic" flavor. Add all the ingredients together in the blender or processor except the evoo, blend well slowly, then add the evoo. The texture will be somewhat grainy because of the pecans and parmesan cheese. The finished product should not be thin or runny. It should not be dry either. If you add to much cheese it will be salty. The pesto should toss evenly with the vegetables coating them well. This salad should be made 1 to 2 days before it is used. It will last only 5 days no more in the fridge before the vegetables start to get mushy. There are several ways to serve this marinated salad.

Buffet style on a beautiful platter or in a serving bowl or as a dinner salad before the entrée. To do this place baby greens on salad plates top with the pecan pesto marinated vegetables garnish with shredded parmesan cheese. Another way is to serve as an entrée salad. To do this use large dinner plates with baby greens or spinach top with the marinated vegetables and chicken. Extra evoo can be poured over this salad for extra flavor. However you enjoy this salad it will be just amazing. Oh! By the way try adding some crushed red chilies to the pesto or jalapenos. You do not like pecans, try almonds, walnuts or any other nut you do like even peanuts. If you like pine nuts try them.

Wanda C. Broccoli & Cauliflower in Sour Crème Tarragon Dressing

Broccoli flowerets
Cauliflower flowerets
Tarragon (fresh or dried)
Ks.
Fgbp.
Sour Crème Tarragon Dressing (recipe follows)

Tarragon again! It is the only herb I have found that I really like with this salad. The taste is just right for broccoli and cauliflower. The broccoli and cauliflower are used raw; if they are cooked the salad will be mushy. Cut the broccoli and cauliflower into flowerets (small bite size pieces with or without some stem attached); mix the dressing combine with the broccoli and cauliflower. This salad will last 4 to 5 days then the broccoli and cauliflower start to break down. This salad is great served with grilled steak or chicken.

Sour Crème Tarragon Dressing

tarragon (fresh or dried)
sour crème
granulated garlic
ks.
fgbp.
tabasco sauce
worcestershire sauce

If you are not a fan of a lot of sour crème, then use 1/2 sour crème and 1/2 mayonnaise. Crushed red chilies or cayenne pepper can also be added for a kick. Fennel either ground, fresh or whole seeds can be added with the tarragon. I use granulated garlic for this salad because it needs garlic but not a strong taste. The granulated garlic is just right powdered garlic can also be used as well as some onion powder or fresh onion. Do not be afraid to add or leave out some ingredients to suit your taste. I suggest you start by using 2 c. sour crème, 1 T. tarragon, 1 t. granulated garlic, salt and pepper to taste. As well as tabasco and worcestershire to taste. Mix well taste then add more of what you want for taste.

Randy Chicken with Pasta in Curry Roast Garlic Vinaigrette

Chicken meat (white or dark)
Pasta (any variety)
Green onion
Grape tomatoes
Curried sunflower seeds (optional recipe follows)
Ks.
Fgbp.
Curry Roast Garlic vinaigrette (*Simply Vinaigrettes)*

It is a long hot day you do not feel like cooking a hot or heavy meal. The pool is calling and the family is hungry. Last night you made grilled chicken with plenty leftover. The night before you cooked pasta with plenty leftover. Simple, last week you made curry roast garlic vinaigrette for dinner with plenty leftover. Looks like a leftover night. Chop or shred the chicken, slice green onions, cut grape tomatoes in half, and combine everything together with the salt and pepper and curry roast garlic vinaigrette. Dinner is served. If you have any lettuce salad it is great tossed in or on the side with this chicken pasta salad. There are plenty of other vegetables that can also be added to this salad to bulk it up if unexpected guests arrive. Maybe fresh berry shortcake for dessert?

Curry Roast Garlic Vinaigrette

4 T. curry powder
4 T. roast garlic (recipe follows)
2 c. unsweetened rice wine vinegar
2 c. evoo
2 c. canola or salad oil
1 t. ks
1 1/2 t. fgbp

There are different types of curry powder, red, green, or yellow, red being the hottest. There is just something about curry and roasted garlic together. The more curry powder you add the hotter the taste. Unsweetened rice wine vinegar? Yes it comes sweetened which is fine if you are combining with rice to roll sushi. Read the labels to make sure there is no sweetener. The label should say natural or original for unsweetened. To make this vinaigrette combine everything together; blend well. If the curry is not hot enough for you try adding jalapenos or cayenne pepper. This vinaigrettes flavor gets better the longer it sits in the fridge. Try it on sandwiches.

How to Roast Garlic

whole garlic cloves in bulbs
evoo

A garlic bulb is what it is called when there is a cluster of garlic cloves all attached. Preheat oven to 350 degrees. The bulbs can be roasted whole or cut in 1/2 across the width. If roasting whole bulbs, place them in the oven and roast for 15 to 20 minutes. They are done when very soft or even mushy. Remove from oven let sit until cool cut off end of bulb squeeze out garlic. To roast bulbs cut in 1/2 place cut side done in pan place in oven for 15 minutes test for softness should be mushy. Let cool squeeze out garlic. To roast peeled whole cloves toss in evoo place in oven for 10 minutes check for softness and mushy if you roast to long the cloves will become hard watch them close after 10 to 15 minutes they burn easy.

Carboni's Curried Sunflower Seeds

1/2 c. raw sunflower seeds
2 T. almond milk
2 t. curry powder

This recipe is from a friend of mine who is also a chef and author. I loved these curried sunflower seeds so much I asked him if I could us his recipe in my book. He agreed. His book is called *Cookin with Carbo* be sure you pick up a copy from Amazon.com. Preheat your oven to 350 degrees. In a mixing bowl, toss the sunflower seeds with the almond milk and curry powder. The almond milk is soy milk. Spray a baking sheet well or use parchment paper spread the sunflower seeds evenly place in the oven. Bake for 6 to 8 minutes; stir after 3 minutes check. At 6 minutes make sure they do not burn. Let cook enjoy.

Linda S. Kidney Bean Salad with Roasted Red Bell Pepper Aioli

Kidney beans
Celery
Red onion
Carrots
Ks.
Fgbp.
Roasted Red Bell Pepper Aioli (recipe follows)

What is an Aioli? It is a dressing or dip made from either mayonnaise or raw eggs. The recipe I use for this salad is made from mayonnaise. I have kept these recipes as simple as I can without losing the flavor. The kidney beans are soft and chewy where the celery, onion and carrots add color and crunch. You can buy dried kidney beans cook yourself or buy canned, already cooked. If you use the canned beans make sure to rinse under cold water drain well. If you cook them yourself make sure you drain well. If you do not, the salad will be watery. To make this salad, first decide which beans you are using. Dice or slice the celery, the red onion can be sliced, diced or julienne and the carrots can be shredded, diced or sliced. Combine everything together with the aioli and serve well chilled. Do not forget to add the salt and pepper. This is another salad that can be served with meatloaf, grilled steak, chicken, fish or seafood. Any of these meats can be added to the salad also.

Roasted Red Bell Pepper Aioli

3 ea. roasted red bell peppers
2 c. mayonnaise (the recipe for making mayonnaise is
    in the recipe for Alicia Curried Chicken)
1 t. ks 1 1/2 t. fgbp
1 T. garlic
1 T. thyme (fresh or dried)

The roasted red bell peppers can be bought already roasted packed in their own liquid (do not throw away the liquid it is great for soups and sauces) or you can roast them yourself. The recipe for roasting red bell peppers is in the recipe for Linda M. Pasta Salad Tossed in Sweet Tomato Vinaigrette. A blender works really great to puree them in. Add the rest of the ingredients blend well. If you do not use all the dressing for the salad, it will keep for about 2 weeks in the fridge.

Marcella Oriental Beef

Beef (leftover steak, pot roast, roast beef are great for
    this)
Yellow bell peppers
Green onions
Sesame seeds (white or black)
Ginger (fresh)
Sesame Vinaigrette (recipe follows)
Ks.
Fgbp.
Crushed red chilies (optional)
Nappa cabbage (optional)

Oriental style salads? Why not? I love oriental food,
don't you? I have 3 in a row all using the same vinaigrette
because it is a great vinaigrette, and that works well with
the ingredients for these 3 salads. If you like, no, love
sesame you will like no love this vinaigrette and salad.
Ever wonder what to do with leftover beef? Make it
into a salad for a pool party or just for a change for
dinner. Beef cooked any temperature will work for this
salad, rare (my personal favorite), medium rare, medium,
medium well, or well done. If you cooked a roast and
it was tough, use it for this salad. The vinaigrette will
tenderize the beef. Making this salad a day or 2 ahead
only improves the taste. This salad will last no more
than 5 days before it needs to be tossed out.

Cut the beef into the shape you want I prefer to use a julienne cut very thin strips about 2 to 3 inches long. Remove the stems, seeds, and membranes from the yellow bell peppers. Cut into julienne strips or dice, and slice the green onions. Red onion can be used instead, sliced or diced. Toast the sesame seeds for added flavor, this can be done 2 ways, use a skillet on the stove, heat it until hot use no oil or pan spray. Add the seeds stir until they are golden brown watch close they will burn fast. If you are using black seeds they will burn without you knowing it, it takes about 2 minutes at the most stirring constantly to toast either one.

The oven method is to preheat the oven to 350 degrees. Put the sesame seeds on a cookie sheet place in oven to toast for maybe 5 minutes. Check if the ones around the outside are turning brown, but the ones in the center are not; then stir them around return to oven for no more than 2 to 3 minutes. The black sesame seeds need only 5 minutes in the oven. Peel the ginger (a spoon works great just scrape the thin skin off , a paring knife or vegetable peeler works great also) the peelings can be used to flavor soups or stocks. Cut the ginger into small pieces then chop the ginger and garlic together. Add all the ingredients together, and toss with the vinaigrette. This salad is great for a salad bar. Nappa cabbage can be tossed in with it for extra flavor and crunch. To serve this salad for a buffet, I like to place it on a large platter, garnish with a small amount of shredded carrot. To serve with nappa cabbage as a buffet salad slice the nappa cabbage very thin. Either toss with the beef salad serve in a large salad bowl or place nappa cabbage on a large platter. Top with the oriental beef salad or place the oriental beef salad in the center of a large platter surround with the thin sliced nappa cabbage. Sesame seeds can be sprinkled over the top to garnish.

Sesame Vinaigrette

2 c. rice wine vinegar
1/2 c. sesame oil
3 c. canola or salad oil
1 t. garlic
1 t. fresh ginger
1 t. fgbp or cbp

Where is the evoo you ask? Not in this vinaigrette. The taste of the evoo overpowers the other flavors. Make sure the rice wine vinegar is the unsweetened unless you want this vinaigrette to be sweet. Put all the ingredients together in a blender or container to use hand held blender; blend well. Crushed red chilies, cayenne pepper, or any chili you prefer can be added.

Chuck R. Oriental Chicken with Rice

Rice (uncooked or leftover cooked)
Chicken (white, dark or leftover)
Zucchini
Carrots
Green onions
Sesame seeds (toasted)
Red bell peppers
Ks.
Fgbp.
Sesame vinaigrette (given in the Oriental Beef recipe)

This salad is a great way to use up the leftover rice from the Chinese takeout the other day, even fried rice. Rice can be white, long grain, short grain, brown, jasmine, basmati, black your choice. Leftover rice is not just for rice pudding anymore. If you cook the rice fresh for this salad prepare according to the directions on the box then add the vinaigrette to the warm rice it will soak in, becoming even more flavorful. The chicken can be leftover baked; grilled, roasted or boiled (I should have named this book *Simple Salads from Leftovers*).

The chicken can be shredded, diced or julienne cut, raw or cooked. It can also be added to the uncooked rice to already cooked or raw to cook with the rice. The zucchini can be peeled or left unpeeled according to your taste. I like to leave the skin on slice length wise into four pieces remove the seeds then slice thin. The carrots should be peeled then either slice very thin or cut into julienne strips, and slice the green onions using the entire onion. Another way is to cut the green onion into 3 inch pieces slice the long way into strings if you place them into ice water for 1 hour at least they will curl up. Toast the sesame seeds until golden brown. The instructions for this are in the recipe for Marcella Oriental Beef. Dice the bell peppers small after removing the stems and membranes. After preparing all the ingredients toss everything including vinaigrette together with salt and pepper. Salads with rice, pasta, and potatoes seem to need plenty of salt and pepper. Slivered almonds can also be added to this salad.

Cory Oriental Noodles with Chicken

Rice Thread Noodles (uncooked)
Chicken (white or dark)
Snow peas
Red bell peppers
Sesame seeds
Ks.
Fgbp.
Mandarin Sesame Ginger vinaigrette (Simply Vinai-
grettes)

What are rice thread noodles and where are they found? They are long thin noodles bought packaged in cellophane in the oriental section of any food store. The package is actually one long thin noodle. To cook them use very hot water about coffee pot hot. If you use boiling water the noodles will dissolve I know this because I did and they did. Place the noodles in a large bowl pour the hot water over the noodles completely covering. The noodles change from an almost white to clear when done. By the time the water gets cold the noodles will be done. They can be broken into smaller pieces before cooking or chopped after. They really have no flavor but take on the flavor of the other ingredients. Make sure to drain well. They can also be fried to do this take from the package using a deep fryer, wok, or large pot with plenty of oil heated but not to smoking. Drop the noodles in the hot oil use tongs to move them around they cook in a flash. They become white and puff up. Drain on paper towel before making the salad. The chicken again can be leftover or fresh cooked in your favorite way. To add more flavor, marinate the chicken in some teriyaki marinade before cooking. Snow peas are found in any food store fresh or frozen with fresh being the best. Remove the ends and strings that run along the flat side. Leave whole or cut in 1/2 or smaller pieces. Remove the stems, seeds, and membranes of the red bell peppers either dice or julienne cut. Toast the sesame seeds the directions for this is in the recipe for Marcella Oriental Beef. Prepare all the ingredients toss together with the mandarin sesame ginger vinaigrette (recipe below). Crushed red chilies can be added as well as jalapenos or other chilies for added flavor. Serve this salad along with egg drop or sweet & sour soup. What a meal! This recipe can also be used with beef, shrimp or pork.

Mandarin Sesame Ginger Vinaigrette

2 c. mandarin oranges with juice
2 t. garlic
1 T. fresh ginger
1 1/2 t. honey
1 c. rice wine vinegar (unsweetened)
1/2 c. sesame oil
1/2 c. evoo
1 c. canola or salad oil
1/2 ks
1 t. fgbp
1 1/2 t. dijon mustard

The fresh ginger and fresh garlic is what really adds to this vinaigrette. The ginger is very easy to peel. Use a spoon or vegetable peeler; the skin can be saved to be used in soups or sauces. Ginger must be cut into small pieces. If it is not, the end result will be stringy. Use the juice along with the mandarin oranges. Combine everything together; blend well. The great thing about mandarin

Oranges is they are already sweet so a sweetener is not needed. The honey is added to enhance the flavors. It goes so well with ginger and garlic. Shrimp is great sautéed with this vinaigrette as well as pork.

Chef Lim Curried Rice with Chicken, Beef or Shrimp

Rice (uncooked)
Chicken, beef or shrimp
Curry powder (yellow, green or red)
Garlic
Red onion
Carrots
Zucchini
Green bell peppers
Evoo
Ks.
Fgbp.

You need not fear curry for it is a beautiful thing. Full of flavor and spice, curry comes in a variety of colors and strengths of heat. Yellow, green, and red are the ones I am familiar with, red being the boldest in flavor and heat. It can be made as mild or as hot as you like. Curry is available in powder or paste forms and is sold at most food stores. The best quality curries are found in stores specializing in eastern Indian cuisine. Curry is not just for rice; it is also great with pasta, potatoes all sorts of meats, poultry, fish and seafood. To prepare this delicious salad cook the rice according to the package instructions with the curry mixed in with the rice and water. Chicken or seafood stock can be used in place of or added to the water; beef stock or base will turn the rice dark in color. Adding the beef raw will also turn the rice ugly. If you are using chicken or shrimp they can be added to the rice raw before cooking as well as the garlic. I recommend this; the flavor is so much more intense. Cut the chicken, shrimp or beef into the shape you prefer—diced or sliced. This is a very colorful salad that is great for potlucks and pool parties. All the salads in this book are best when served very cold; most of them are better if made several days ahead. The red onion can be diced small or large, julienne cut, or left in thin rings. The carrots should be peeled. It is one vegetable that the skin is not good left on in a salad, unless you are cooking them. They are great skin-on and cooked with a beef roast or roasted chicken. The zucchini can be used peeled or not; the green of the peel adds color. You can also leave the seeds in or removed. The zucchini can be diced or thin sliced, the green bell peppers after removing the stems, seeds and membrane can be sliced or diced. After preparing all the ingredients to your liking toss them all together with evoo, salt and pepper. The evoo is used to moisten and add flavor to the salad. It gives it a beautiful shine. Curry goes well with evoo. If you have a specialty store in your area try using some harrisa evoo or another flavor. Nuts can also be added to this salad at the end or cooked with the rice. Dried fruits such as apricots, pineapple, or cranberries can also be added at the end. Any of these oriental salads can also be served vegetarian style with vegetables such as mushrooms, bean sprouts, or bok choy added. I do not cook any of the vegetables in this salad because the crunch adds so much.

Megan Rice with Chicken, Beef, Shrimp or Pork in Cumin Honey Vinaigrette

Rice (cooked or uncooked)
Chicken, beef, shrimp or pork (cooked or uncooked)
Peas
Carrots
Zucchini
Greens onions
Celery
Cilantro
Ks.
Fgbp.
Cumin Honey Vinaigrette (Simply Vinaigrettes)

Another salad made with rice? One of the nice things about rice is that there are many varieties to choose from brown, basmati, jasmine, long grain, short grain, black etc. It is good for you and easy to cook. If you do not have any leftover from the other night then cook some fresh. Some rice cook with equal amounts of water to rice and some are 2 parts water to 1 part rice, so read the instructions for the rice you choose to use. Add the vinaigrette to the rice while it is still hot, but be careful when doing this. The hot rice will soak up the vinaigrette making for a more flavorful salad. Chill it while you are preparing the rest of the ingredients.

The chicken, beef, shrimp, or pork can be leftover or fresh cook for this salad. If you are using raw product, I suggest marinating it in some of the vinaigrette for 4-6 hours before cooking in your favorite way. I use frozen peas when making this salad they will not mush when mixed and will be thawed before you use the salad, fresh peas can also be used as well as snow peas. The carrots can be sliced, diced, or shredded. I like to leave the zucchini skin on cut in 1/2; remove the seeds and slice thin. Slice the green onions very thin as well as the celery, it adds a nice crunch if you are not a celery fan leave it out. When it comes to the cilantro, I like to use the whole leaf just pick off the stems make sure to wash it first sometimes cilantro is grown in sand. Add everything together with the rice vinaigrette mix, toss well, and serve well chilled. This is another salad that is even better with crushed red chilies, jalapenos, cayenne pepper or even habaneros.

Cumin Honey Vinaigrette

1 T. cumin seed
1 T. ground cumin
1/4 c. honey
1 1/2 t. dijon mustard
1 c. apple cider vinegar
1 c. evoo
1 c. canola or salad oil
1/2 t. ks
1 t. fgbp

The cumin seed needs to be toasted. To do this, heat a skillet until hot and add cumin seeds. Stir until toasted. This should only take less than 2 minutes. Do not leave unattended it will burn fast. Let the toasted seeds cool before adding the other ingredients; blend everything well together. This vinaigrette is great on salads made of cabbage and or pasta.

Alicia Curried Chicken

Chicken (cooked or uncooked)
Curry powder
Celery
Green onions
Mayonnaise (recipe follows)
Tabasco sauce
Worcestershire sauce
Garlic
Ks.
Fgbp.

Yes I like curry! No I love curry! You will also after you try this salad. The curry with the creamy texture of mayonnaise along with the celery crunch, chicken, the green onion, garlic, tabasco, and worcestershire sauces—what a taste! Extra pepper especially if it is cracked black pepper only makes it better. Go easy on the salt a little will do. If you are using raw chicken, I suggest that you make a marinade of curry powder, and garlic with a small amount of canola or vegetable oil. Coat the chicken let it marinade for 3 to 24 hours; then cook in your favorite way. Let it chill then dice or julienne cut the chicken. Slice or dice the celery, slice the green onions, chop the garlic toss together with the chilled chicken. In a separate bowl combine the mayonnaise, tabasco, worcestershire, and salt and pepper blend well; toss with the chicken mixture. Blend everything together well. Serve well chilled. This salad can be kept in the fridge for 5 days. Ways to serve this salad are as a sandwich on a toasted bun or roll with a side salad or as an entrée salad tossed with or served on top of baby greens, spinach or cabbage. Also fresh or ground ginger, jalapenos, or crushed red chilies can be added for more flavors.

Homemade Mayonnaise

Yields 1 1/2 c.
1 egg yolk
1 t. dry mustard
1 t. sugar
1/2 t. ks
2 T. lemon juice or vinegar
1 c. salad oil

Use an electric mixer. Separate egg, use egg white for other cooking. Combine egg yolk, mustard, sugar, 1/2 the lemon juice or vinegar and salt, whip on high until white and creamy; slowly add salad oil 1 T. at a time continually whipping until ½ of the oil has been added. Add rest of oil while still whipping then slowly add the rest of the lemon juice or vinegar. Continue whipping until it has all been added. This will keep for 2 weeks in the fridge.

Tye Pecan Chicken

Chicken (cooked or uncooked)
Celery
Green onion
Tabasco sauce
Worcestershire sauce
Pecans (halves or pieces toasted)
Mayonnaise (fresh made or processed)
Ks.
Fgbp.

Pecans and chicken? They are made for each other! The soft texture of the chicken along with the crunch of the pecans—especially if you toast the pecans—when eaten together is delightful to the palet. This is a great way to use leftover chicken; it can be boiled, baked, roasted, or grilled. When using fresh cooked chicken, always make sure it is cold before adding the mayonnaise. Adding it to the warm chicken could cause the salad to spoil more rapidly. To toast the pecans, preheat the oven to 350 degrees, place the pecans on a cookie sheet or in a pie pan and place in the hot oven. Check after 5 minutes if they are toasting around the outside edges and not in the center; stir and then return to the oven for no more than 2 minutes and check again. They should be nicely toasted. Make sure they are completely cooled before adding to the salad.

The celery can be cut into thin slices or diced it is your choice, the green onions can be sliced thin or thick; add the tabasco and worcestershire sauces to your taste. Yes, I do use a lot of tabasco and worchestershire sauces—they add a lot of flavor. The same with the mayonnaise (the recipe to make your own mayonnaise is in the recipe for Alicia Curried Chicken). You may like a lot or a little; the choice is yours. I always go easy on the salt and add lots of black pepper.

Mix this all together refrigerate then enjoy. A nice way to serve this salad is in a hollowed out pineapple. To make the hollowed pineapple, select a firm but not hard pineapple. Leave the leaves on the top and stand on end. Start at the very top of the leaves be careful the tips are sharp and like to poke fingers. Use a sawing action with a serrated knife all the way down the pineapple until it is cut in half. Lay halves on flat surface and cut side up using a paring knife cut along the edge between the meat and skin. Make sure you go completely around the inside of the pineapple, being careful not to cut thru the skin. Run the knife down both sides of the core in the center carefully remove the pineapple meat from the skin. After the meat is out, run the knife under the core. Remove and either toss away or chew on it. The core is fibrous but full of juice. The core can be boiled with water, juice or herbs to make a base for pineapple chicken soup. Soups! That sounds like another recipe book. The pineapple cut from the shell can be diced added to the salad or tossed with baby greens or spinach to serve with the pecan chicken salad. To serve the chicken salad in the pineapple, simply fill the shell with the salad. It looks beautiful on a buffet in the center of a large serving platter surrounded by baby greens or spinach with the pineapple pieces. More pecans can be scattered over the top.

Trista Tortellini with Vegetables

Tortellini (frozen, dried or fresh)
Carrots
Zucchini
Red onion
Broccoli
Cauliflower
Red or yellow bell peppers or both
Ks.
Fgbp.
Red Wine Vinaigrette (Simply Vinaigrettes)

Tortellini—what beautiful pasta! This pasta comes in a variety of styles. There is dried, fresh, frozen, plain white, spinach or other vegetable flavored, filled with cheeses, meats and vegetables. After you have decided what style you are using, follow the manufacturer's directions to prepare. The only exception I make is if I use frozen I do not cook it I use it right from the package frozen. This is because tortellini is very delicate mashes and breaks apart easy. The frozen is usually precooked, so you're good to go. If you use a style that needs cooked be careful when cooking do not stir too much drain then toss with the vinaigrette while the pasta is still hot. This will cool it down some and prevent it from sticking together. Let this cool completely before adding the rest of the ingredients. To prepare the vegetables, peel then slice the carrots. zucchini can be peeled or left skin-on, whole, sliced, diced, or cut in half then sliced. The red onion is nice julienne cut, the broccoli and cauliflower can be sliced thin or cut into florets, the bell peppers I like to julienne cut. Toss the vegetables with some of the red wine vinaigrette before adding to the tortellini; it makes it easier to toss. Beef, chicken, or pork are great added to this salad to make a complete meal as well as pepperoni and salamis. To serve this salad, I like to use a large pasta bowl. Shredded parmesan cheese can be sprinkled over the top to garnish.

Red Wine Vinaigrette

1 c. red wine vinegar
2 c. evoo
1 T. sugar
1 T. garlic
1 T. fresh or dried basil
1 T. fresh or dried oregano
1 T. fresh or dried thyme
1 T. dijon mustard
1/2 t. ks
1 t. fgbp

Yes there are a lot of herbs in this vinaigrette. I like a lot of herbs in vinaigrettes. To blend this vinaigrette simply combine everything together; blend well. Try using this vinaigrette on sautéed, steamed or grilled vegetables or even baked potatoes, fried potatoes, roasted or boiled.

Tracey Southwest Cottage Cheese Salad

Cottage cheese
Tomatoes
Cilantro
Green onions and or red onion
Cumin (ground)
Coriander (ground)
Cayenne pepper
Ks.
Fgbp.
Jalapenos or habaneros (optional)

Have you ever wondered what to do with cottage cheese besides just eat it plain? It is a very versatile food. Besides being made into a southwest style salad, it can also be made with curry or fresh ginger and added to chicken; the list is endless. This salad is very fast and simple to prepare. It will last about 6-7 days in the fridge. Start by deseeding and dicing the tomatoes. Clean the cilantro leaves off the stems. Either leave them whole or chop. Slice the green onions thin. If you use red onion fine dice it; if you prefer, grind the cumin and coriander seeds yourself or use already ground. Toasting them first intensifies the flavor. The directions for toasting cumin and coriander seeds is in the recipe for Cumin Honey Vinaigrette is in the recipe for

Megan Rice with Chicken, Beef, Shrimp or Pork in Cumin Honey Vinaigrette. All seeds toast the same way. The cayenne pepper should be added in moderation; more can be added after mixing and tasting. I do not use a lot of salt, cottage cheese has plenty already but do add a lot of black pepper. The jalapenos are an optional addition other dried or chopped chilies can be added for extra zing. This is another salad that is great served in a pineapple shell or hollowed out honeydew, cantaloupe or even watermelon it is also a great side dish for barbeque chicken or pork. No matter how you serve it you will never look the same at cottage cheese. Evoo can also be added to this salad for taste and shine.

Chris N. Cabbage & Apple

Cabbage (nappa, green head, etc.)
Apples (red, green or both)
Lemon water (enough to coat apples)
Red onion
Pecans (chopped or halves untoasted)
Poppy Seed dressing or Poppy Seed vinaigrette (recipes
    follows)

More cabbage? Why yes, there are so many different varieties and flavors. Green head cabbage has the strongest flavor. Nappa looks like fine lace and is sweeter. I like to use a blend of nappa and green head sliced very thin. The apples are fine diced or shredded. If shredding, peel first; the skin does not shred. If diced, the skin can be left on. After shredding or dicing the apples toss with the lemon water to keep from turning brown as fast, once the apples are tossed with the dressing they will be fine. If you prefer toss them with some of the dressing instead of using lemon water. Drain well if using lemon water. Peel then dice or julienne cut the red onion toss with the cabbage. The pecans can be chopped or left in halves; save some for the top after plating. Toss everything together with the poppy seed dressing of your choice. I give 2 recipes below—a version made with mayonnaise and a version made with vinegar. To serve this salad, place in a large serving bowl or platter top with the leftover pecans.

Almonds or walnuts can also be used in place of the pecans. This salad needs to set for a day or so before serving so the flavors can come out. Chicken can also be added as well as pork, pineapple, or even dried fruit. Crushed red chilies or jalapenos are a nice touch also as well as curry.

Poppy Seed Dressing (Mayonnaise Version)

2 c. mayonnaise (recipe for making your own is in the recipe for Alicia Curried Chicken)
1 c. poppy seeds
1 c. sugar
1 c. cider vinegar (for a milder taste apple juice can be used)
1/2 c. red onion
1/2 t. ks
1 t. fgbp

Onion again! Actually I think onion adds a lot to poppy seed dressing. The red onion should be fine diced unless you are going to put in a blender or use a hand held blender to mix. Simply put everything together blend with a wire whip until well mixed if you are not using a blender or hand held blender. If you make your own mayonnaise, this dressing will be good for 2 weeks only; if using processed mayo, it will last a lot longer. There are so many preservatives in the commercially processed mayo, the onion will make this dressing go bad before the mayo.

Poppy Seed Vinaigrette (Vinegar Version)

2 c. cider vinegar or half vinegar half apple juice
1 c. poppy seeds
2 c. sugar
1 c. red onion
4 c. canola oil
1/2 t. ks
1 t. fgbp

Measure all the ingredients; blend together well.

Nate H. Macaroni Salad

Macaroni
Celery
Green onions
Cucumber
Red bell peppers
Mayonnaise Dijon mustard dressing (recipe follows)
Ks.
Fgbp.

Every buffet salad recipe book must have a macaroni salad in it. This book is no exception. Macaroni salad goes with summer picnics like mustard with hot dogs. There are as many different macaroni salad recipes as there are pastas. This is my favorite; the dijon mustard just gives it the right taste. Cook your macaroni until it is done then rinse in cold water to rinse off the starch and stop the cooking. Dice the celery, green onions and bell peppers. The cucumbers can be either peeled, unpeeled, seeded or seeds left in sliced or diced. Toss everything together with the mayonnaise dijon mustard dressing make sure to add salt and pepper. Another dressing that is very good on macaroni salad is thousand island dressing or thousand island vinaigrette (my mock thousand island dressing recipe from *"Janie's Simply")* is given below, thousand island vinaigrette is in the recipe for Grandma Ikie Thousand Island Chicken Salad).

Mayonnaise Dijon Mustard Dressing

I do not give a quantity for each ingredient because it depends on your taste and how much you need to make.

mayonnaise (fresh made or processed the recipe for making your own is in the recipe for Alicia Curried Chicken)

dijon mustard

tabasco sauce

worcestershire sauce

ks.

fgbp

Combine everything together; blend well, and adjust the taste to suit yours. Start with 1 T. of dijon for each cup of mayonnaise the dijon will overpower everything if you are not careful yes the name is mayonnaise dijon but too much of either is not good.

Mock Thousand Island dressing

I do not give quantities for this dressing either it
    depends on your taste
mayonnaise (fresh made or processed)
ketchup
sweet pickle relish (dill pickle can be used instead)
ks.
fgbp.
tobasco sauce
worcestershire sauce
white onion (optional)

Combine all the ingredients together, blend well,
and adjust to taste.

Richard E. F. Peas & Cheddar

Green peas (frozen or fresh uncooked)
Cheddar cheese (yellow or white)
Buttermilk Chive dressing (recipe follows)

This is a wonderful spring time salad. Great for the first cookout of the season. Why use frozen peas? Canned or fully cooked peas have that cooked not crisp taste and mush when mixed. Fresh peas raw right out of the garden are great for this salad also. Leave the peas in the freezer until the last minute after the rest of the ingredients have been mixed together. The cheese can be either diced or shredded. I like the look of this salad when the cheddar cheese is diced; it looks great with the round peas. Toss the cheese together with the dressing mixing. Mix well. Now add the frozen peas. Mix well again. This salad will last no more than 7 days before the cheese breaks down. If you do not like mayonnaise, there is a cayenne pepper vinaigrette recipe in the entrée salad section of this book in the recipe for Mary Lou Spinach, Figs & Cheese.

Buttermilk & Chive Dressing

chives (fresh or dried)

mayonnaise (fresh made or processed the recipe to make is in the recipe for Alicia Curried Chicken)

sour cream

buttermilk

cayenne pepper

ground cumin

garlic powder

onion powder

tabasco sauce

worcestershire sauce

ks.

fgbp.

Combine all the ingredients together for the dressing. If you make too much, do not worry; it can be used for other salads. It is great on leftover baked potato salad. If you use fresh chives, chop fine. Dried are good to go. Add all the ingredients together, blend well, and adjust the flavor to suit your taste. Go easy on the cumin and cayenne pepper; more can be added.

Ardis Cabbage, Cucumbers, & Green Bell Peppers

Green head cabbage
Carrots
Green bell peppers
Cucumbers
Sweet Tarragon Red Wine Vinaigrette (recipe follows)
Ks.
Fgbp.

The secret to this salad's taste is to slice everything as thin as possible. If you have a food processor, that is perfect. Peel the carrots before slicing. The bell peppers can be left whole or sliced; just pick out the membrane or cut off top remove seeds and membrane then slice very thin, the cucumbers can be peeled or left unpeeled, left whole sliced very thin or cut in1/2 the long way. Remove seeds and slice very thin. To prepare the cabbage cut in quarters remove core slice very thin. Toss everything together with the vinaigrette; let marinate a day or so before serving. This salad looks really great on a large platter. This is another great salad to serve with a grilled steak or pork chops. There are so many other foods that can be added to this salad such as nuts, mushrooms, and onions, just to mention a few.

Sweet Tarragon Red Wine Vinaigrette

1 c. tarragon vinegar
1 c. red wine vinegar
1 c. sugar or sugar substitute
1 t. tarragon (fresh or dried)
4 c. canola oil
1 T. dijon mustard
ks.
fgbp.
2 t. garlic

If you really like tarragon like I do, use 2 c. tarragon vinegar instead of the red wine vinegar. Combine everything together; blend well. This vinaigrette is also great as a marinade for chicken, pork, or beef to use with this salad.

Richard F. Green Beans with Dill

Green beans (fresh or frozen)
White onions
Cider vinegar (hot not boiling)
Garlic
Dill weed (fresh or dried)
Cayenne pepper
Ks.
Fgbp.
Boiling water (to blanch beans)

What better way to use all those fresh green beans that are available in the summer along with the beautiful white or vidalia onions that are so plentiful and delicious. This recipe can also be used for canning green beans. Yellow beans are very good this way also. Bring a large pot of water to boil to blanch the green beans, heat the vinegar until warm, cider vinegar can also be added straight from the bottle not heated I find the flavor infuses with beans better when warm. Slice or dice the onions, slice thin or chop the garlic. If using fresh dill pull leaves off stems chop or leave whole, dried dill is good to from the bottle. Combine the onions, garlic, dill, cayenne pepper, salt and pepper together in a large bowl. Blanch the green beans for 1 minute take from the boiling water do not rinse drain well add to the onion mix, slowly add the warm vinegar, being careful not to breath in too hard. It is always a good idea when pouring hot or warm liquid to keep your face and head back. I know when I breath it in by accident it takes my breath away, and that can be bad. Let this set at room temperature until it is cool enough to cover and refrigerate. Let this set in the fridge for 3 to 4 days then enjoy. If you do not like cayenne pepper then use jalapenos or another chili of choice. If you do not like chilies or spice then leave it out sugar can be added instead to make it sweet and sour, these beans are great for a tossed salad or a side dish to a grilled steak. Small leftover amounts can be added to cooked potatoes or pasta to make another delicious and surprising salad.

Matt H. Julienne Meats & Cheeses

Swiss cheese
Cheddar cheese
Monterey jack cheese
Smoked ham
Turkey (smoked or roasted)
Salami (hard or soft)
Roast beef
Dill pickles
Red bell peppers
Green bell peppers
Red onion
Cbp.
Cider vinaigrette (*Simply Vinaigrettes*)

The only thing I can say about this salad is that if you are not hungry when you start preparing it, you will be by the end due to all the different cheese and meats with their smells and tastes. I do not know of any cheese or meat that would not be great in this salad. Dill havarti, smoked gouda, provolone, or mozzarella—the list of cheeses is endless. As for the meats there are different hams and salamis. The list is endless, and they are all great in this salad. The way the cheeses and meats are cut is up to you—dice or julienne. If I dice the cheese, I julienne cut the meats. I usually dice the pickles. If they are bought as wedges, I just slice them into bite size pieces if I buy whole pickles I cut into round slices gherkins can also be used (small baby dill or sweet pickles). There are also different types of pickles, bread and butter, sweet, hot and spicy or kosher dill just to name a few. I like to use plain dill pickles. To prep the bell peppers cut off the stems remove the membranes and seeds slice or dice, peel the onions slice or dice them. No matter how you cut everything the salad is beautiful. Toss everything together with the cider vinaigrette and enjoy do not forget the cracked black pepper. I avoid adding any salt there is plenty in the meats and cheeses. Hot peppers can also be added for extra flavor. This salad should be discarded after 5 days. The cheeses do not hold up; they start to break down. This salad is great served on a salad bar with baby greens and or fresh spinach on the side or tossed in. Split a large sub roll spread with some of the cider vinaigrette toast on a hot grill or on a griddle. Load up the sub roll with plenty of the salad top with sliced tomatoes and baby greens or spinach enjoy. Pasta can also be added to this salad to make a more complete meal.

Cider Vinaigrette

1 c. cider vinegar
1 c. evoo
1 c. salad, canola or vegetable oil
1 1/2 t. dried or fresh basil
1 1/2 t. dried or fresh oregano
1 T. dijon mustard
1 1/2 t. sugar
1 1/2 t. garlic
1 t. fgbp
1/2 t. ks.

Combine all the ingredients together; blend well. The uses for this vinaigrette are endless.

Shawna H. Tarragon Marinated Baby Corn

Baby corn
Red bell peppers
Green onions
Ks.
Fgbp.
Tarragon Vinaigrette (recipe follows)

Talk about a simple salad! They do not get any simpler than this one. Full of flavor and color. The baby corn is in a can or jar with liquid just open the can or jar and drain. The liquid can be used as the base for a soup or sauce; it does not really have any corn taste. It is water and salt. Slice the tiny ears of corn down the center from tip to end into 2 pieces. Remove the stems, membranes and seeds from the bell peppers dice fine, the green onions are sliced from tip to end. Toss everything together and let marinade for several days in the fridge before serving. This is another great salad that is good served as an item on a salad bar. Chicken or shrimp can be added as well as cayenne pepper or jalapenos.

Tarragon Vinaigrette

1/2 c. tarragon vinegar
2 t. tarragon (dried or fresh)
1 c. canola or salad oil
1 c. evoo
2 t. garlic
1/2 t.ks
1 t. fgbp
1 t. dijon mustard

Why do I use dijon mustard in so many of these recipes you ask? It is like the egg in the cake it holds everything together. *Emulsifies* is the term. The vinaigrette can be made without the dijon; it will be fine. It just will not stay together as well. Sometimes they do not stay together no matter what you use to emulsify. I talk about xantham gum in the introduction. It is the best emulsifier I have found, but it does not always hold everything together. To make this vinaigrette place everything together in a blender or container; blend well. This vinaigrette will keep for a long time in the fridge. Just shake, pour, and enjoy.

Ben Southwest Three Bean

Pinto beans
Black beans
Green beans (fresh, canned or frozen)
Nopalitas cactus
Jicama
Jalapenos (fresh or canned)
Red bell peppers (roasted)
Red onion
Ks.
Ffbp
Red Wine Cilantro Vinaigrette (recipe follows)

What are nopalitas cactus and jicama? Are they eatable? How do you prepare them? Do you have the answers? I do! Nopalitas cactus is bought at any store selling Mexican food items. They are the pads of the nopalitas cactus and can be bought already prepared in jars with this slimy liquid that you discard. They are delicious, soft and chewy with a very mild taste. Just open the jar drain use (do not rinse in water that will lose some of the flavor). In some areas of the country, mostly the southwest, the cactus pads can be bought uncleaned with the thorns attached. I know; I have done this. It's awful and painful. The pads need to be steamed until tender; then the pads should be scraped to remove thorns. Thick leather gloves need to be worn to do this. Take my word for it, buy them already done.

Jicama is a root vegetable native to the southwest and México. They have a thin skin that is easily peeled off with a paring knife or vegetable peeler. Jicama is crunchy and sweet, taking on the taste of what you mix it with. I like to cut the jicama into julienne pieces about 1 inch long.

The pinto beans and black beans can be bought already cooked or you can purchase them dry and cook. If you use canned make sure you rinse well if you do not the salad will be cloudy. The green beans can be fresh, frozen or canned. I prefer to use fresh or frozen. When using fresh blanch for 2 minutes or when they are done, put in ice water to stop the cooking. I like green beans to have a little snap, but when they squeak between my teeth they need cooked longer. Frozen green beans have already been blanched cook longer if you prefer. Canned are okay, but sometimes they are done too much. The jalapenos can be diced fresh, canned, diced, sliced, pickled— it's your choice. If you buy fresh, cut off stem end and remove seeds and membranes; then fine dice. The jalapenos can also be blended into the red wine cilantro vinaigrette. The red bell peppers can be bought already roasted or you can roast them yourself. The recipe for roasting red bell peppers is in the recipe for Linda M. Pasta Salad Tossed in Sweet Tomato Vinaigrette. If you buy them already roasted, but do not rinse them. That will remove most of the flavor. Save the liquid for soups and sauces. Julienne cut or small dice the roasted red bell peppers. Peel the red onion dice large, small or julienne cut. The nopalitas, jicama, red onion and jalapenos can also be roasted or grilled for more flavor. Mix everything together, add the salt and pepper, and toss carefully with the red wine cilantro vinaigrette. Be careful; if you toss or stir too hard, the beans will mash. Serve this salad well chilled. Grilled chicken or steak can also be added to this salad. Jalapeno, roasted red bell pepper or cayenne pepper vinaigrette can also be used for this salad.

Red Wine Cilantro Vinaigrette

1 c. red wine vinegar
1 c. evoo
1 c. canola, salad or vegetable oil
1 c. cilantro (fresh or dried)
1 T. sugar
1 T. garlic
1/2 t. ks
1 t.fgbp

Red wine vinegar and cilantro? Won't the red wine vinegar over power the cilantro taste? No it will not. I use enough cilantro that will not happen. Cider vinegar can be used instead for a milder vinegar taste. To make this vinaigrette, start by rinsing the cilantro in cold water to remove any dirt or sand still on the leaves. Pat dry, remove the leaves from the stems. Combine everything together; blend well. Try using this vinaigrette on sautéed, steamed, or grilled vegetables or even baked potatoes, fried potatoes, roasted potatoes, or boiled potatoes. A small amount of xanthan gum can be added for thickening.

Pat H. Simple Coleslaw

Green cabbage
Carrots
Green onions
Green bell peppers
White onion
Simple Cole Slaw Dressing (recipe follows)

Not only does every good buffet salad recipe book have a three bean salad they also have a good coleslaw recipe. At least I think this one is good; it gets eaten every time I make it. This is a great salad for a hot, late night cookout. I use green cabbage only for this one; it is easy to work with and is hearty. This salad will hold up in the fridge for a week. Start out by slicing the cabbage very thin. Everything in this salad is sliced very thin. The carrots should be peeled first; not peeling them can make the salad dark in color. After everything is sliced, toss together in a large bowl with the dressing. Chicken or pork can be added to this salad to make a nice dinner entrée salad served on a large dinner plate with warm crusty bread.

Simple Coleslaw Dressing

mayonnaise (fresh made or processed the recipe is in the recipe for Alicia Curried Chicken)
sour cream
sugar
vinegar (cider or white)
ks.
fgbp.

To make the dressing mix the mayonnaise, sour cream, sugar, vinegar, salt, and pepper together until well blended. I use 2 parts mayonnaise, 2 parts sour cream to 1 part sugar and 1 part vinegar; the salt and pepper are to taste. If you prefer a vinegar and oil on your slaw but want it creamy, replace most of the mayonnaise with any oil you prefer, (evoo, canola or vegetable oils). A combination of evoo and canola or vegetable oil with a small amount of mayonnaise gives a nice creamy change. Poppy seeds, caraway seeds, or celery seeds can be added as well as dried red pepper flakes or cayenne pepper.

Shawn F. Bleu Cheese, Broccoli & Cauliflower

Broccoli flowerets
Cauliflower flowerets
Bleu cheese crumbles
Red onion
Ranch dressing (mixed)
Fgbp.

Ranch dressing? I bet you thought I did not know what ranch dressing was? Not my favorite! I do not even have it in my house. Kids really love this salad and will eat it up. If you do not like ranch there are many vinaigrettes that are great with this salad. Bleu cheese vinaigrette is fantastic, roasted red bell pepper, Creole, jalapeno, and cilantro vinaigrettes just to name a few. The recipes for these vinaigrettes are in my recipe book, *Simply Vinaigrettes*. There are also several vinaigrettes in my recipe book, *Janie's Simply Entrée Salads*, that are great in this salad—sweet French or sweet Italian vinaigrettes just to mention a few. Of course most of these recipes are used in this book somewhere. This salad is really very fast and easy to put together. Make it the day before so all the flavors can blend or marry as the term is. Start out by cutting the broccoli and cauliflower into florets—small, bite size pieces. Julienne cut the red onion, crumble the bleu cheese, and combine everything in a mixing bowl. Then add the pepper and ranch dressing. (I do not add salt because there is plenty in the ranch mix and bleu cheese). Toss well to mix. Store in a closed container and keep refrigerated. This salad will last about 5 days no more the vegetables break down. I recommend serving this salad with grilled steak, pork, or chicken even burgers. Another great flavor to add to this salad is bacon, cook crisp crumble in with the vegetables add the ranch tossing well.

Cookie Steak & Potato Salad

Steak (grilled, baked, prime rib, pot roast or even leftover)
Potatoes (baked, boiled, grilled, roasted, fresh cooked or leftover)
Green onions
Bell peppers (red, green or yellow or any combination)
Ks.
Fgbp. or cbp
Dijon vinaigrette *(Simply Vinaigrettes)*

This salad is a great way to use up that leftover beef you have been wanting to use. Pork or chicken can also be used but of course then it would be Cookie Pork & Potato or Cookie Chicken & Potato. Leftover meats and potatoes really soak up the vinaigrettes very well. I found that if I reheated the meat and potatoes then tossed them with the vinaigrette right from the oven, the vinaigrette broke down. They need to be at room temperature or well chilled, I cut the meat and potatoes into bite size pieces and then slice the green onions from tip to end. Remove the stem, seeds, and membranes from the bell peppers; dice smaller than the other ingredients. Toss everything together well with the salt, black pepper, and vinaigrette. Add a spinach salad with sweet red onion vinaigrette *(Simply Vinaigrettes)* tomatoes and mushrooms along with a good cold dark beer. *Wow*! What a dinner. Maybe a fresh fruit cobbler for dessert? Another great vinaigrette for this salad is Honey dijon vinaigrette the recipe follows.

Dijon Vinaigrette

1 c. dijon mustard
2 c. cider vinegar
2 c. canola or salad oil
2 c. evoo
1/2 t. ks
1 t. fgbp or cbp
1 T. garlic
1/2 t. crushed red chilies (optional)

Combine everything together; blend well. You may want to make extra. This vinaigrette is great with a lot of sandwiches and salads.

Honey Dijon Vinaigrette

1 c. dijon mustard
1 c. honey
1 T. fresh or dried thyme
2 t. garlic
1 t. ks
1 1/2 t. fgbp or cbp
2 c. salad oil
1 c. cider vinegar

Put all the ingredients together; blend well.

Keith Red Skin Potato Salad

Red skin potatoes
Green onions or red onions
Celery
Ks.
Fgbp.
Mustard Potato Salad Dressing (recipe follows)

To peel or not to peel? The answer is yours. I myself never peel potatoes I cook. The skin is very thin and easy to chew. To slice or dice? There again the answer is yours. I like to dice them. To cut potatoes before cooking or after? The answer is yours. I like to cut them first. If I am cooking red skin potatoes for dinner the night before and know I want potato salad sometime in the next 3 days, I cook more. To boil, oven roast, or put on the grill in foil? Why in foil? If they are put on the grill without foil or in a pan, the chance of them burning is greater; burnt potatoes are not good anytime. Guess what? The answer is yours. I have no preference on this. After you have decided how you are going to cut the potatoes and have cooked them, make sure they are cool so you can safely handle them. While the potatoes are cooking prep the onions. To slice or dice? You are right; again, the choice is yours. For me the green onions need to be sliced using the whole onion from end to end, the red onions I either julienne or dice, to slice or dice the celery? Yes, your choice. I like to slice very thin like done for Asian cooking. After the potatoes have been cooked and cooled put them in a large mixing bowl, add the onions and celery, add the salt and pepper, and then the dressing mix well. Refrigerate and serve well chilled. To add hard cooked eggs or not? Keep in mind a lot of people have allergies to eggs. For me it depends on my mood. This is the perfect salad for a cook out with burgers, dogs, and brats.

Mustard Potato Salad Dressing

sweet pickle relish
mayonnaise (fresh made or processed the recipe for this
    is in the recipe for Alicia Curried Chicken)
yellow or dijon mustard
tabasco sauce
worcestershire saucc
ks.
fgbp. or cbp

Some people like there potato salad dressing very heavy or light on their salad. I give no quantities for this recipe because how much you want depends on how much you need to make. Also some like there's heavy mayonnaise taste or heavy mustard. I mix this dressing to taste. Put all the ingredients in a bowl mix well adjust taste for salt, pepper, tabasco sauce and worcestershire sauce. Also some people like there's sweeter than some add more sweet pickle relish.

Kailee Feta Cheese & Mushrooms

Shitake mushrooms
Button mushrooms
Artichoke hearts
Feta cheese crumbles
Roasted garlic cloves
Ks.
Fgbp.
Oregano vinaigrette (recipe follows)

Never, ever wash mushrooms. By this I mean do not run them under water or let them sit in water. Mushrooms are like a sponge and soak up water like one. If they need some cleaning wipe by hand with a damp cloth. The same with strawberries. I remove the stems before I slice, dice, or cook the mushrooms. Do not toss them away; use the stems in sauces and soups. Grill or roast the mushrooms for this salad. Roast the mushrooms by tossing in some of the oregano vinaigrette; place on a cookie sheet or in a roasting pan in a 350 degree preheated oven for no than 15 to 20 minutes. They will burn very easy. If you are grilling mushrooms, do so your usual way. I roast the garlic separately. It takes a little longer to roast than the mushrooms, and it just adds another level of flavor (the directions for roasting garlic is in the recipe for Randy Chicken with Pasta in Curry Roast Garlic Vinaigrette). To prepare the button mushrooms, cut them in 1/2 or

1/4, slice or cut the shitake mushrooms depending on their size; really small mushrooms I leave whole. If you are grilling the mushrooms cut after being careful they are hot. Toss the mushrooms and roasted garlic with more oregano vinaigrette while they are still warm. Let this cool down before adding the artichoke hearts and feta cheese. The reason I let it cool before adding the artichoke hearts and feta is because the artichoke hearts will fall apart and the feta cheese will melt and clump. The artichoke hearts can be cut in 1/2 or 1/4 the feta cheese crumbled or cut in cubes. Go easy on the salt because of the cheese but do not be stingy with the pepper. This is another salad that is even better with cracked black pepper. Red pepper flakes can be added as well as cayenne pepper or even chipotles. If you do not like feta cheese try using blue cheese, havarti, swiss, or even cheddar. Lemon juice can also be added for a zing. Fresh lemons of course.

Oregano Vinaigrette

2 T. fresh or dried oregano
2 c. cider vinegar
4 c. evoo
1 T. garlic
1/2 t. ks
1 t. fgbp

Garlic infused evoo can be used in place of the evoo and garlic. Combine everything together; blend well.

There are so many other great uses for this vinaigrette. Marinate chicken, pork, beef, or seafood before grilling but do not marinate for more than 6-8 hours. This vinaigrette is also great for salads made with pasta, potatoes, rice, or cabbages.

Vicki Homney & Roast Corn

Homney
Kernel corn (fresh on cob, frozen or canned)
Red and green bell peppers (roasted)
Green chilies (hot, mild, fresh or canned roasted)
Pepper jack cheese
Garlic
Ks.
Fgbp.
Sweet Oregano Vinaigrette (recipe follows)

If you use fresh corn on the cob (my favorite way), pull the husks back remove the silks coat the kernels in oil either evoo or salad oil pull the husks back up over the kernels either roast or grill in your favorite way. The corn can still burn if left to long or not watched closely. After roasting or grilling let cool cut the kernels off the cobs. Homney is bought canned. It is large white or yellow kernels of corn already cooked in the can. Rinse and drain well to remove any residue on the kernels this will cause your salad to be cloudy. Place the corn and hominy in a large mixing bowl; remove the stems, membranes and seeds from the bell peppers. Slice or dice and add to the corn and hominy. Do the same with the fresh green chilies. The bell peppers and fresh green chilies can be roasted first the directions for doing this are in the recipe for Linda M. Pasta Salad Tossed in Sweet Tomato Vinaigrette. Bell peppers and chili peppers hot, sweet, or mild roast the same. Roasting really brings out the flavors making any recipe better. The pepper jack cheese can be either shredded or diced add to the other ingredients along with the garlic add the salt and pepper toss everything together then add the sweet oregano vinaigrette mix well again. Cooked chicken or beef can be added to this salad, especially if it is marinated in the sweet oregano vinaigrette before grilling or roasting. Do not keep this salad for more than 5 days; the cheese breaks down and is not nice to look at or eat.

Sweet Oregano Vinaigrette

2 c. cider vinegar
1/2-1 c. sugar
1 T. oregano (fresh or dried)
2 c. salad oil
2 c. evoo
1/2 t. ks
1 t. fgbp

If you are wondering, apple cider vinegar and cider vinegar are the same. They are made from apple cider. Combine all the ingredients together using 1/2 c. of the sugar to start blend taste add more sugar if not sweet enough. Artificial sweetener can also be used.

George Ratatouille

Eggplant
Zucchini
Yellow squash
Red onions
Red yellow and green bell peppers
Basil (fresh)
Garlic
Evoo
Roma tomatoes
Ks.
Fgbp.
Shredded parmesan cheese

This is one of those dishes that can be served hot or cold. It is great either way. I do not peel the eggplant, zucchini, or yellow squash, but you can peel them if you prefer. They cook well and are easy to chew. Preheat oven to 350 degrees. Dice the eggplant, zucchini, yellow squash, and red onion. I do not remove the seeds from them either except the roma tomatoes. All the vegetable for this dish are cut into bite size pieces. Remove the stems, membranes, and seeds from the bell peppers dice. Cut the roma tomatoes in 1/2; remove the seeds and dice. Remove the basil leaves from the stems; chop coarsely. If you are using fresh garlic cloves, cut each clove into about 4 pieces and toss everything together except the cheese including the evoo (just enough to coat well not enough to make it oily) and salt and pepper. Mix well and place in a baking dish in preheated oven for 10 minutes. Remove and stir well return to oven for 10 more minutes remove from oven let come to room temp stir in cheese. I like to serve this salad in a large pasta bowl garnished with more shredded parmesan cheese and fresh basil leaves either whole or chopped. Another way to serve ratatouille is to place on oven toasted slices of thick French bread. Slice the bread thick, generously butter on both sides, place on cookie sheet in the oven under broiler or with the oven set on 450 degrees, toast, but do not burn. Turn to toast other side. Place ratatouille on toast top with shredded parmesan cheese place back under broiler or in oven until cheese bubbles. Serve with a side salad of spinach with red onion drizzle with good balsamic vinegar enjoy. Besides drizzling the spinach salad with the balsamic. Also try drizzling some on the ratatouille whether it is cold or hot. Add a glass of a good red wine. Maybe cheesecake or tiramisu for dessert.

Crystal M. Ham, Cheddar, &Dill Pickles

Ham
Sharp cheddar cheese
Dill pickles
Sweet pickle relish
Fgbp.
Honey Mustard Dressing (recipe follows)

What a combination! Where does she get these ideas! Well! Most of them I come up with just driving in my car either to work or home. I either start by combining foods then think of a vinaigrette or dressing, or I come up with a vinaigrette or dressing then start putting food combinations together. Do I ever come up with something I would not feed my family? I would be untruthful if I said no. Now on to this delicious salad. When it comes to the ham I want one with lots of smokey taste. Bone in, boneless or picnic ham either works. I peel the rind off they are very chewy in a salad. Do not throw it away; save it for ham and beans, same with the fat. With a bone in, you will have thick rind with lots of fat. A boneless or picnic ham there will be no fat or should be no fat. After peeling the ham, dice in bite size pieces and put in a mixing bowl. The cheddar can be diced or shredded your choice. If you do not like sharp cheddar than use mild cheddar, colby, Monterey jack, jalapeno jack, havarti, swiss and even velveeta if that is your idea of cheese. I have also used more than 1 kind of cheese to make this salad more interesting. There are so many different types and flavors of cheeses to choose from even imported specialty cheeses. I stay away from soft cheeses like brie or soft goat cheese. Dill pickles! Well there are a variety of them to choose from take your pick. Sliced, spears, whole, gherkins (baby or cocktail pickles available sweet or dill as they are sometimes called). I usually use the spears or whole, if I use spears, I cut them into bite size pieces if I use whole I cut them into spears then cut into bite size pieces. Add the pickles to the ham, add the sweet relish and pepper I do not add any salt there is plenty in the cheese, ham and pickles, toss well with the honey mustard dressing. This is what I call a sweet and sour salad. Baby greens, spinach or arugula can be tossed in or placed on a plate topped with the ham, cheddar and dill pickle salad.

Honey Mustard Dressing

mayonnaise (homemade or processed the recipe for making this is in the recipe for Alicia Curried Chicken).
honey
dijon mustard
ks.
fgbp.

If you use 2 c. of mayonnaise add 1/4 c. honey, 2 T. dijon mustard, salt and pepper to taste. Mix this well taste then adjust flavor for your liking. Want more honey flavor? Add another 1/4 c. Want more of a mustard taste? Add 1 T more. Need more salt and pepper? Well, add small amounts and mix well again. Keep doing this until you have the flavor you are seeking. I do not like mayonnaise, so I go heavy on the dijon and pepper. For extra flavor try adding a few drops of tabasco and worcestershire sauces.

Mike M. Pasta Primavera

Pasta
Red or white onion
Red, green and yellow bell peppers
Cucumber
Broccoli
Carrots
Cherry or grape tomato
Olives (black, green, or kalamata)
Cheese (any variety)
Garlic
Basil (fresh or dried)
Oregano (fresh or dried)
Evoo (flavor infused are great)
Vinegar (optional; your choice of rice, cider, red wine, balsamic flavored or traditional)
Ks.
Fgbp.
Herb Creamed Italian Dressing (optional recipe follows this dressing is also in *Simply Vinaigrettes*)

Pasta primavera is a meatless pasta dish. I have given you some suggestions for vegetables to put in this salad. There are plenty of other vegetables available. When it comes to cheese for this salad the choices are endless. It depends on what taste you are looking for. Sometimes I use bleu cheese, dill havarti, gouda, feta, swiss, or provolone. I stay away from soft cheeses such as soft goat cheese. The vegetables can be diced, sliced, or julienne cut. The cherry or grape tomatoes can be cut in 1/2 as well as the olives. Let's talk olives. There are more varieties than what I mention. In the ingredients, the choice is yours. I always like to use a lot of fresh chopped garlic. This can be blended with the evoo along with the salt, pepper, basil, and oregano. If you have one of those awesome stores near you with the flavored balsamics and evoo's from around the world, that is even better. They are the best for pasta salads. You say you want a creamy vinaigrette for this pasta salad? I have given the recipe for mine following this recipe. To make this salad after cooking the pasta go from the pot to ice water with it to stop the cooking. This is called shocking the pasta. Drain the pasta well place in a large mixing bowl. While the pasta is cooking, cut the vegetables the way you want them. Add to the pasta and toss well; then add thc cheese or cheeses (yes I said cheeses; you can have more than 1 or 2). If you are using the evoo, vinegar, garlic and herbs blended together; pour over pasta, vegetables, and cheese. Toss well and do not forget to add the salt and pepper. Serve this salad well chilled; discard any unused after 5 days.

Herb Creamed Italian Dressing

1/2 c mayonnaise (fresh made or processed the recipe
    to make is in the recipe for Alicia Curried Chicken)
1 c. cider vinegar
1 c. salad, canola or vegetable oil
1 c. evoo
1 1/2t. garlic (fresh or dried)
1 1/2 t. oregano (fresh or dried)
1 1/2 t. basil (fresh or dried)
1 1/2 t. thyme (fresh or dried)
1 T. dijon mustard
1/2 t. ks
1 t. fgbp

Combine all the ingredients together; blend well
with a blender or hand blender. This dressing will last
about 2 weeks in the fridge. This dressing is great on an
Italian submarine sandwich or hoagie.

Mamma Maddux Sun Dried Tomato Pasta

Pasta (any kind)
Sundried tomatoes
Parmesan cheese
Pine nuts (toasted the recipe for this is in the recipe for Tye Pecan Chicken)
Basil (fresh)
Evoo
Ks.
Fgbp.

This is one of those pasta salads that does not have a vinaigrette, just fresh basil, evoo, and garlic. A flavored evoo would be excellent. Some that come to mind would be lemon, basil, wild mushroom, and harrisa—well, you get the picture. The pasta selection you make should be cooked until well done, do not be afraid to use spaghetti or linguini. Sundried tomatoes come either packaged dry or packed in evoo. If you use the dry packaged I suggest soaking them in hot water for at least 10 minutes to soften unless you like the chewy texture right from the package. The ones packed in evoo are already soft just cut into julienne strips or chop. Use the evoo from the sundried tomatoes in your salad. The parmesan cheese can be purchased already shredded or grated you can also purchase a chunk shred, grate or chop yourself. Pine nuts are just that little nuts from the pine cones (they do taste like pine) not my favorite. My suggestion is if you are not sure you will like pine nuts, taste one before toasting, and taste one after toasting. Then if you still do not like them, use another nut or none at all. Sunflower seeds would be good. They can be toasted also.

All nuts toast the same 350 degree preheated oven for 5 minutes only (they burn fast) or in a sauté pan on the stove until toasted golden brown. This only takes a few minutes. The basil can be sliced or fine chopped; the garlic if you use whole cloves can be sliced very thin or chopped. Do not use too much garlic the taste will be very bitter on your tongue not pleasant. To make this salad, simply toss all the ingredients together with the salt and pepper. Adding cooked chicken or Italian sausage to this salad makes a great lunch or dinner with some good wine and crusty bread.

Frank Orange Slaw

Fresh oranges
Green cabbage (nappa or head)
Red onion
Sugar or artificial sweetener
Ks.
Fgbp.
Mayonnaise (fresh made or processed the recipe for
    this is in the recipe for Alicia Curried Chicken)
Lemon juice

This salad is a great side dish with fish, seafood, or pork. It is also great served on a corned beef sandwich or a good kosher beef hot dog. The type of cabbage used is your choice. I prefer nappa cabbage; it is lighter in flavor lacy in looks with a slightly sweet taste. No matter what your choice of cabbage is slice it very thin (purple cabbage can also be added be sure to rinse it well if you do not your salad will be pink). The oranges should be peeled with all the white removed; it will make the salad bitter. Use a paring knife to cut sections out between the membranes (when cut this way the orange sections are called supreme) or leave the sections attached chop into bite size pieces. Orange sections can be bought already done. Peel and then fine dice the onions. Combine the oranges, cabbages, and onions together in a mixing bowl. In another bowl, combine the sugar, salt, pepper, mayonnaise, and lemon juice together and mix well. Add this dressing mix to the cabbage, oranges, and onions and mix well. This slaw is great served in a large serving bowl lined with cabbage leaves. Toasted nuts such as almonds can be sprinkled on top to garnish. To make this salad a complete meal, just add grilled tuna, shrimp, chicken, or smoked sausage.

Nancy B. Cranberry Cashew Chicken

Chicken meat (white, dark, boiled, baked, grilled or leftover)

Dried cranberries (the recipe to make your own dried cranberries is in the recipe for Grandma Ikie Thousand Island Chicken all fruits dry the same)

Cashews (whole, chopped, toasted or untoasted the recipe to toast nuts is in the recipe for Tye Pecan Chicken).

Cranberry Sage Vinaigrette, Cranberry Vinaigrette, or Cranberry Pesto (recipes follow)

If you love cranberries like I do, then you will love this salad. If you are not a cranberry fan, try using dried cherries or both. It is the perfect salad for a Thanksgiving or Christmas buffet. All the ingredients have a different texture when you take a bite of this salad. They all go together so well. Some people prefer to soak the dried cranberries in hot water for about 10 minutes to soften them. I do not. They are not tough, and I like the chewy texture they have. Prepare the chicken in your favorite way. Mine is grilled. Cut into bite size pieces and add dried cranberries and cashews. I do not chop the cashews. I like them whole. If you prefer them chopped, buy them that way or chop yourself. I have found that chopping cashews small causes them to get lost in the chicken salad; I want them to be seen well too. Combine all the ingredients together with the vinaigrette or pesto mix well. Make sure to serve this salad well chilled. This salad is even better if it is made the day before. It can also be used as an entrée salad just by placing it on top of some baby greens serving more vinaigrette or pesto on the side or drizzle over the top. If you do not like cashews, try walnuts or almonds. Some crushed red chilies or jalapenos can be added for extra flavor and kick.

Cranberry Sage Vinaigrette

1/2 lbs. fresh cranberries or 1 can jellied or whole canned cranberries
2 t. dried ground or fresh sage
2 c. canola, salad or vegetable oil
1 c. cranberry or rice wine vinegar
1 T. dijon mustard
1/4 c. sugar
1/2 t. ks
1 t. fgbp

I prefer to freeze the cranberries first before blending into vinaigrette, they blend smoother. It makes a lot of noise, but it is worth it. To make this vinaigrette, simply combine everything together; blend well.

Cranberry Vinaigrette *(Simply Vinaigrettes)*

Use the recipe for Cranberry Sage Vinaigrette, just leave out the dried ground or fresh sage.

Cranberry Pesto

1 1/4 c. dried cranberries
1 c. pecans or cashews (untoasted)
1/4 c. shredded parmesan cheese
1/2 tsp. fgbp
sage or any other herb is optional
evoo
canola, salad or vegetable oil

You are probably wondering why I do not give quantities of oils. The amount of each oil you use depends on how moist you want your pesto to be. Some prefer a dryer version, some a moister. You are also probably wondering why I am not using all evoo as pestos are supposed to be. With fruits in most cases, if I use all evoo, to me it takes over the flavor of what I am making. I want to taste the fruit first then the oils. I also did not add any herbs or garlic because the taste was what I wanted without them. They certainly can be added. I am not a salt lover. I feel there is enough salt taste from the cheese, but if you want to add some, by all means do. To make this pesto, simply put everything except oils in a food processor or blender and blend well, slowly adding oils until desired consistency.

Joe J. Ham & Bean Salad

Great northerner beans
Smoked ham
Carrots
Celery
White onion
Garlic
Ks.
Fgbp.
Thyme Vinaigrette (recipe follows)

If you love ham and bean soup this salad is for you. I have taken all the ingredients that make a great ham and bean soup except the broth. I replaced that with a vinaigrette and turned it into a great buffet salad. If you use canned beans, rinse them well. If you cook your own, drain them well and make sure they are cold so they will not mush when tossed. Pick a well-smoked ham. I prefer to use either picnic or bone in. I stay away from the chopped, formed, want-to-be ham. I use a ration of less ham then beans about 2 parts ham to 3 part beans. Cut the ham into small pieces, the carrots can be julienne cut, diced or chopped small, the celery can be diced or sliced thin, and the garlic needs to be chopped fine, small dice the onion. Prepare the beans, ham, carrots, celery, and onions; put in a large mixing bowl and go easy on the salt, but load on the pepper. Pour the thyme vinaigrette over the ham and beans mixture toss carefully so you do not mash the beans. Ham and bean salad needs to marinade for 2-3 days before serving for the best flavor and will last 6-7 days no more. This is another salad that chilies of some sort can be added for flavor and kick. To serve this salad, place in a large serving bowl and garnish with some fresh thyme.

Thyme Vinaigrette

2 T. fresh or dried thyme
4 c. canola, salad or vegetable oil
1 T. garlic
2 c. cider vinegar
1 T. dijon mustard
1 t. ks
1 1/2 t. fgbp

If you have noticed, I do not use evoo for this vinaigrette for this salad. I feel the evoo taste tends to take over the taste in this salad. That does not mean you cannot add it. I want you to taste all the ingredients, not just the evoo. Combine all the ingredients together; blend well. This vinaigrette is also great on pasta with chicken or beef.

Grandma Ikie Thousand Island Chicken

Chicken (white, dark, baked, broiled, boiled, grilled, roasted leftover)
Celery
Dried cherries (recipe follows)
Candied walnuts (recipe follows)
Thousand Island Vinaigrette or Mock Thousand Island Dressing (both are in *Janie's Simply Entrée*)

For those of you who are real thousand island fans, this is for you. I created the thousand island vinaigrette for my husband to get him to eat more vinaigrettes. The flavor of the thousand island vinaigrette is light and fresh. This salad is a great way to use leftover chicken. Here you are using leftover foods again! Your family and friends will never know. Your secret is safe with me; I will not tell anyone. The chicken can be sliced, diced or shredded. Celery is simple slice or dice. To finish this salad, prepare all the ingredients and toss them together with the thousand island vinaigrette. Get ready for a special treat. To serve for a buffet, place in a nice large serving bowl, garnish with more dried cherries and candied walnuts. To serve as an entrée salad, serve on top of baby greens or spinach on large dinner plates or salad bowls garnished with more dried cherries and candied walnuts. If you do not like dried cherries try blue berries, apricots, pineapples, or even dried apples. If you do not like walnuts, try almonds, cashews, or pecans.

Thousand Island Vinaigrette

1/2 c. chili sauce
1/4 c. sweet pickle relish
2 c. canola, salad or vegetable oil
1/2 c. red onion
1/2 c. rice wine vinegar
1/2 t. ks
1 t. fgbp
1/2 t. worcestershire sauce
1/2 t. tabasco sauce

When I first created this recipe, I used ketchup. The next time I used chili sauce. The flavor is much more there. Where do you find chili sauce? In the grocery aisle with steak sauces, worcestershire sauce, etc. To make this simple vinaigrette, peel the onion and cut in quarters. Put in a container or blender with the rest of the ingredients and blend well. I have not found any salad either buffet or entrée that this vinaigrette does not make better. Some of my coworkers had doubts, until I tossed some with fresh berries. They were convinced. I added some jalapenos to this vinaigrette to make a fiery thousand island vinaigrette. Need I say *wow*? The recipe for mock thousand island dressing is in the recipe for Nate H. Macaroni Salad.

Dried Cherries

The dried cherries are good to go right from the package. Of course, if you dry them yourself, it is even better. To do this, either use a food dehydrator or your oven. Wash the fresh cherries in cold water, remove the pits from the cherries, and place on the trays of the food dehydrator following manufacturer directions. To do them in the oven, preheat oven to 250 degrees, wash and pit cherries, and place the fresh cherries on baker's racks on cookie sheets in the oven to dry. This may take at least 12 hours or longer to dry. I like to dry food in the oven overnight. There is no set time for any dried foods in the oven or dehydrator. It depends on the moisture content which will vary from one piece to another. Drying foods myself is fun and healthier, but takes a lot of time. Most dried foods bought are coated with a sugar or sweetener of some sort and or a salt product.

Candied Walnuts

Candied walnuts add a nice, sweet crunch. To make candied nuts (they all are done the same way) use 1 egg white for each cup of nuts. Preheat oven to 350 degrees. Separate the egg and save the yolk for baking. In a mixing bowl, add egg whites, 1 t. cayenne pepper, and 1 T. sugar. Mix with an electric mixer or wire whip until almost the consistency of meringue. Add the nuts mix well place on a sprayed cookie sheet place in oven for 5 minutes. After 5 minutes, check if nuts are still very moist; then return to oven for no more than 3 minutes. Remove from oven and hide so you and your family do not eat them before the salad is made. You may want to make extra to store in a zip lock bag to keep crisp for later use.

Wynema Bleu Strawberry Pasta Salad

Rigatoni pasta
Green onions
Grape or cherry tomatoes
Strawberries
Chicken (great way to use leftover)
Pistachios (toasted, untoasted or candied)
Bleu Cheese Strawberry Vinaigrette (recipe follows)

Bleu cheese, strawberries, and pasta? Wow! What a flavor explosion. Add the green onions, tomatoes, and pistachios. Wow! Wow! You notice I do not have any bleu cheese in the salad ingredients. That is because there is plenty in the vinaigrette. I love bleu cheese, but too much is just that—too much. Add some to the salad mix if you want to. You can also sprinkle some over the salad after it is bowled before serving. I chose rigatoni because they cook really well. The vinaigrette gets into the center of the pasta. Why green onions? I love their taste with strawberries and tomatoes. I prefer grape or cherry tomatoes; they are sweeter. Why pistachios? Why not? They keep their crunch and again go well with strawberries, tomatoes, and green onions. Here is how I make this delicious treat. I will not bore you with the usual bring lots of salted water to a boil. Cook the pasta until done, drain put in ice water to stop the cooking. Drain well again put in a large mixing bowl. While the pasta is cooking slice the green onions all the way from tip to end, slice or 1/4 the strawberries, dried strawberries are great also sweet and chewy (the directions for how to dry fruit is in the recipe for Grandma Ikie Thousand Island Chicken, the only difference between strawberries and cherries is there are no pits. Cut them in half or slice dry the way you choose). Cut the tomatoes in 1/2 or slice, sliced grape or cherry tomatoes are really nice in a salad. The pistachios can be left whole or chopped, toasted, untoasted or candied. The directions for toasting nuts is in the recipe for Tye Pecan Chicken, the recipe for candied nuts is in the recipe for Grandma Ikie Thousand Island Chicken. No matter how the chicken is cooked for this salad, it can be shredded or diced. Make sure the chicken is cold when adding to the rest of the ingredients the vinaigrette will break (separate) the results will be a unattractive salad. Combine everything together toss well with the vinaigrette be careful not to smash the strawberries. To serve place in a large serving bowl garnish with bleu cheese, pistachios or more strawberries or all of these. If you do not like pistachios try pecans or walnuts instead.

Bleu Cheese Strawberry Vinaigrette

1 c apple cider vinegar or 1 c. apple juice or 1/2 c. of each
1 c. strawberries (fresh or individual frozen)
1 c. bleu cheese
1 c. salad, canola or vegetable oil
1/2 t. ks
1 t. fgbp

Why can I not use strawberry jam or those cooked frozen strawberries? You can but you will not like the end result it does not look appetizing. This vinaigrette is so easy to make if you want it real creamy blend the bleu cheese in with everything else. If you want the vinaigrette chunky with bleu cheese, blend everything together except the bleu cheese crumble in by hand stir with a spoon. More bleu cheese can be added for your taste. Crushed red chilies are really great in this vinaigrette as well as cayenne pepper or habaneros. Also this vinaigrette gets better as it sits in the fridge I suggest making it at least 4-7 days ahead place in a closed container in the back of the fridge forget until you are ready to use.

Pat P. A Blast of Fruit

6 c. Baby greens
1 ea. Pear
1 ea. Peach
1 ea. Plum
1 ea. apricot
1 ea. Apple (red or green)
1 ea. Mango
1 ea. Papaya
1 ea. Kiwi
1 c. Walnuts (toasted)
2 ea. 6oz. Chicken breast or tuna steak
1 c. Plum Vinaigrette (recipe follows)

This salad is as much a blast to make as it is to eat. All the fruits are fresh and can be used peeled or unpeeled except the kiwi. The skin on the kiwi is fuzzy and not a pleasant taste bitter. The skin on the papaya is thick and chewy but can be eaten if you choose. The fruits can be used sliced, diced or both. The pear, peach, plum, apricot, papaya, and apple can be cut in half then remove the seed. The seeds from the papaya can be toasted. To do this preheat the oven to 350 degrees place the seeds in a pan in the oven toast for 5 minutes, they take on a nutty taste us them to sprinkle over the salad. The mango has a large flat seed in the center. This seed is usually 1/4 to 1/2 inch thick. Lay the mango on the side run the knife down the side of the seed cutting off the meat. There is a ring of meat left on the seed use a paring knife remove the rest of the meat from the seed. The mango meat can be cut off the skin easily using a paring knife cut the meat in the skin cutting top to bottom and side to side push up on the bottom of the skin turning it inside out cut the meat off the skin into bite size pieces. The skin on the mango can also be peeled off with a peeler or paring knife making it possible to slice the meat into julienne pieces. Mix all the fruits together with the vinaigrette this can be done a day ahead. The walnuts can be toasted for extra crunch and flavor this really brings out the oils in the nuts. All nuts are toasted the same way the directions for how to toast nuts are in the recipe for Tye Pecan Chicken. Walnuts take on a glossy look this is the oil being released from the nuts. As they cool they lose the glossy look. I like to serve this salad in large salad bowls. As with most of my entrée salads, I recommend grilling the chicken breasts or tuna steaks. Another suggestion is to marinate them in the plum vinaigrette for 4-12 hours than bake or broil. To prepare this salad I toss the baby greens and fruits together in the plum vinaigrette place in the salad bowls top with the chicken breast or tuna steaks scatter the walnuts over the top then drizzle with more of the vinaigrette. Another way to serve this salad is to place the baby greens in the bowls add the fruits then top with the chicken or tuna add the nuts drizzle with the vinaigrette or serve the vinaigrette on the side. The chicken or tuna can also be tossed with the baby greens and fruits before placing in the salad bowls. If you are not a walnut person there are plenty of other nuts or even sunflower seeds can be used. Beef steaks can also be used.

Plum Vinaigrette

2 c. plums or plum preserves
2 T. thyme (fresh, frozen or dried)
1 c. cider vinegar
1 c. evoo
1 c. canola, salad or vegetable oil
1 T. dijon mustard
1/2 t. ks
1/2 t. fgbp

Yes you can use fresh plums, frozen plums or plum preserves equal amounts of any. Put everything together in a blender or container for using a hand held blender; blend well.

Ludella Pepperoni Pasta

6 c. Linguini

1 c. Pepperoni

1 c. Arugula

10 ea. Grape tomatoes (red or yellow)

1 c. Smoked Gouda cheese

1 c. Provolone cheese

1 c. Black olives

1 c. Green olives

2 ea. 6oz Chicken breasts or 12oz dark meat

1 c. Roasted Red Bell pepper Vinaigrette *(Simply Vinaigrettes)*

Who does not have a good pasta salad? This one has it all flavor, texture and color. The roasted red bell pepper vinaigrette really finishes the flavors off very nicely. Other pastas can also be used. In fact this is a great way to use leftover spaghetti, fettuccini or tortellini. The pepperoni can be left whole, sliced or diced. I have even used the mini pepperoni in this salad. The chicken can be cut in strips, diced, shredded, grilled, baked, broiled, boiled or leftover the choice is yours. If you are grilling chicken for this salad I suggest marinating it for 4-12 hours in some of the roasted red bell pepper vinaigrette before grilling. Arugula is actually a herb used like lettuce. If the leaves have a yellow tint that is okay the taste of arugula is peppery. The grape tomatoes can be used whole or cut in half, during the summer season when tomatoes are in season I suggest using any variety available. If you use large tomatoes cut in half remove seeds dice. The cheese can be diced, julienne cut or shredded. The black and green olives can be cut in 1/2. The green onions I slice using the whole onion from tip to end. This salad can be plated using large dinner plates or pasta bowls. I like to toss everything together place on the plates or in the bowls. A sprinkle of shredded parmesan cheese can be added for garnish. Another way to plate this salad is to place the pasta on the plates or in the bowls add all the ingredients then pour the vinaigrette over the top. This salad can also be made in a large quantity for a buffet. There are other vinaigrettes that are great for this salad such as roasted red bell pepper chipotle vinaigrette to make this add some chipotle chilies to the roasted red bell pepper vinaigrette blend well. Creole or sweet red onion vinaigrettes *(Simply Vinaigrettes)* are also very good with this salad. Another vinaigrette that is great on this salad is sweet tomato vinaigrette the recipe for this vinaigrette is in the Linda M. Pasta Salad Tossed in Sweet Tomato Vinaigrette.

Roasted Red Bell Pepper Vinaigrette

3 ea. red bell peppers or 1 c. roasted red bell peppers
1 t. garlic
1 c. red wine vinegar
1 c. evoo
1 c. canola or salad oil
1 t. dried oregano
1/4 t. ks
1/2t. fgbp

The directions for roasting red bell peppers are in the recipe for Linda M. Pasta Salad Tossed in Sweet Tomato Vinaigrette. The roasted red bell peppers can also be bought packed in jars at the store. Peel the garlic and combine everything in a container or blender. Make sure you blend well sometimes roasted bell peppers take a little more blending. You will find lots of uses for this vinaigrette such as putting on deli sandwiches or mixing with mayonnaise for a dip or spread. Raw vegetables are also great dipped in it.

Martin Very Berry Coconut Shrimp

2 c. Baby greens
2 c. Romaine lettuce
2 c. Iceberg lettuce
1 c. Blue berries
1 c. Strawberries
1 c. Red onion
2 c. Coconut (1/2 toasted 1/2 untoasted)
12 ea. Raw shrimp (size 21-25)
1 c. Tangerine Tarragon Vinaigrette *(Simply Vinaigrettes)*

If you like sweet, berries, coconut and shrimp this is your kind of salad. The red onion adds the right touch of snap. I choose baby greens, romaine and iceberg lettuces for their flavors and textures. Romaine and iceberg can be bought already cut or cut them yourselves. The strawberries can be cut in quarters or sliced. The red onion I like to dice small. The coconut can be processed bought from the store or a whole fresh coconut. To use fresh coconut there are 3 indents on the coconut use either a drill or a screwdriver with a hammer. Make at least 2 holes pour out the coconut flavored water, do not throw it away drink, mix with fruit juice, use to make Jell-O, cake batter well you get the idea. After you have drained the water out use the hammer to break open the coconut you can toast the coconut meat in the shell then remove or remove chop or grate then toast. Toast 1/2 of the coconut the other 1/2 is for coating the shrimp. Coconut toasts the same way as nuts, so preheat the oven to 350 degrees spray a cookie sheet well, spread the coconut on the cookie sheet place in the preheated oven for no more than 5 minutes. If the coconut is toasting around the edges stir from outside edge inward return to oven for no more than 2 min. Remove from oven and let cool completely. The shrimp I use is size 21-25. Shrimp are sized by how many it takes to make a pound. The larger the shrimp the lower the count number. So 21-25 in a pound raw. This salad really looks nice on large dinner plates especially if they are black or red. The shrimp can be bought at any grocery stores frozen section. Yes you can buy already coconut breaded shrimp in some freezer sections of some stores. But making them yourself is more fun and tastier. Thaw the shrimp in cold water or in fridge overnight. If you thaw in fridge rinse well before breading. This is where you will use the untoasted coconut. Heat frying oil or vegetable to 350 degrees. Never use extra virgin olive oil to fry foods only to sauté in small quantities. You will need a dish of flour with salt and pepper, 2 eggs whipped with 1 T. water (this is called egg wash), 1 dish of untoasted coconut. The reason you need the coconut untoasted for breading is because it will burn faster if already toasted. The thawed shrimp can be left whole or butterflied. To butterfly lay shrimp on a cutting board on its side tail toward you. Start with a sharp paring knife cut the back open from tail to head end not cutting all the way through then spread open dip in flour then egg then coconut, until all 12 are breaded. If you want a long piece of shrimp slice all the way through then open full length hold by one end bread just like butterflied shrimp. The breading can be done a day or 2 before using just cover with plastic place in fridge until used. Extra shrimp can be done at the same time frozen raw for later use. When you are ready to fry, carefully place in hot oil fry until golden brown. Remove from oil place on paper towel to drain. To assemble the salad cut the iceberg and romaine lettuces, toss with the baby greens add the berries, onion and coconut toss with the tangerine tarragon vinaigrette. Place in the center of large dinner plates add the shrimp placing 6 on each plate. More vinaigrette can be drizzled over the shrimp. This salad will soon become one of your favorites. It is great for a hot summer night by the pool, bridal or baby shower. Chopped nuts such as almonds can be added to the untoasted coconut.

Tangerine Tarragon Vinaigrette

2 oz. tangerine juice or puree

1 c. tarragon or apple cider vinegar

1-3 T. sugar

1 T. dijon mustard

1 c. evoo

1 c. canola or salad oil

1/2 t. ks

1 t. fgbp

Combine all the ingredients together except the sugar start by adding only 1 T. blend well taste add more sugar as you prefer. You can always add more sugar but you cannot take it away. You will have to increase all the other ingredients before you know you have a gallon. I know I have.

Mary Lou Spinach, Figs, & Cheese

6 c. Fresh spinach
8 oz. Soft goat cheese
8 oz. Soft sheep cheese
6 ea. Fresh figs
1 c. Walnuts (toasted or candied)
2-8oz. Beef steaks
1 c. Cayenne Pepper Vinaigrette *(Simply Vinaigrettes)*

Figs! Fresh figs with cheese? Not just any cheese! Goat cheese and sheep cheese! With fresh spinach, a beef steak, cayenne pepper vinaigrette and walnuts? This could be interesting and tasty! Where do I find fresh figs, goat cheese and sheep cheese? Most food stores anymore have a great cheese and produce sections. Goat cheese and sheep cheese come in many different forms plain soft, smoked, herbed, even with sundried tomatoes. There is not a form of either cheese that will not go great with this salad. Make your choice and enjoy. Fresh figs may be hard to find they are seasonal, but they are worth the hunt. My grandmother and great grandmother grew them in their yards. I would never try them I thought they would not be good. Never crossed my mind they were what fig newton's are made of boy do I love them. I sure missed out on a lot of years of yummy. If you use fresh spinach bought in bulk, wash it in clean cold water and drain well; either pat dry or spin dry to remove the water. Never leave it to soak in the water, spinach soaks up water causing it to not last as long in the fridge. Spinach is grown in sandy soil a lot of times and not washed well. The directions on how to toast nuts is in the recipe for Pat P. A Blast of Fruit. The directions on how to candy nuts is in the recipe for Grandma Ikie Thousand Island Chicken. Should I toast or candy the nuts? They both bring a lot to the party it depends on if you want sweet and crunch or just crunchy. My steak of choice for this salad is a lean sirloin marinated in the cayenne pepper vinaigrette 4-6 hours before grilling. I like to use large dinner plates for this salad. Start by placing the fresh spinach in the center of both plates, crumble or dice the cheese scatter over the spinach, the figs do not need to be peeled or deseeded they are completely edible. Cut them into bite size pieces scatter over the plate, add the walnuts. After grilling the steaks slice place over the salad then drizzle everything with the cayenne pepper vinaigrette. This salad can also be served with everything including the steak tossed in the vinaigrette. If you are not a fan of cayenne pepper or any chili peppers at all then I suggest cilantro vinaigrette or a fruity vinaigrette such as blackberry thyme or sweet cherry all 3 of these are in my recipe book *(Simply Vinaigrettes)*.

Cayenne Pepper Vinaigrette

2 T. cayenne pepper
1 T. dijon mustard
1 c. cider vinegar
1 c. evoo
1 c. canola, salad or vegetable oil
2 t. garlic
1/2 t. ks
1 t. fgbp

If you are not sure if this will be too hot for you start with 1 T. cayenne pepper more can be added but not taken away. 1/2 t. of honey can be added or 1/2 t. of sugar can also be added for a little sweetness. Put everything together; blend well. The longer this vinaigrette sets in the fridge the better the flavor is. All vinaigrettes only improve with time.

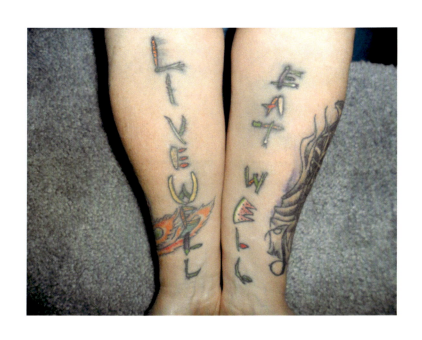

160 | Janie Ebinger

Janie S. Fire Roasted Fruit & Chicken

6 c. Baby greens
8 Slices pineapple
8 Slices honeydew
8 Slices cantaloupe
2 ea. 6 oz. Chicken breasts
1/2 c. Strawberries
1/2 c. Blue berries
1/2 c Raspberries
1 c. Almonds (toasted or untoasted)
2 c. Pineapple Cinnamon Vinaigrette

If you have never experienced grilled honeydew, pineapple or cantaloupe just wait until you do! Wood or charcoal fire! Which is better? Some prefer wood some charcoal. The choice is yours. At my house we use only wood. We have a grill made for wood. I always start my cooking fire with fire starter not lighter fluid. The taste of the lighter fluid always gets into my food. Fire starters can be bought at most stores or you can make your own. All you need is cardboard egg cartons, sawdust, and candle wax. After I wrote these directions I said to myself, "When was the last time you saw a cardboard egg carton"? Well! When I went to the grocery store later that day I realized they do not exist anymore unless you buy the 5 dozen case. If you buy the cardboard 5 dozen eggs case then you have them. Place the sawdust in each compartment of the egg holder, carefully and slowly melt wax, old candles are great for this do not leave this unattended it will catch fire easy. When the wax is melted carefully pour over the sawdust in the egg cartons let set 2 days to harden. If you camp a lot you will love them. They can also be made water proof by cutting each cup apart carefully dip them into the melted wax let harden. Store in a closed waterproof container. Another method of fire starter is to use the 2 oz. bathroom disposable paper cups. For this you will need 2 oz. cups, sawdust, string, and melted wax. Cut the string in about 4 inch pieces place in cups fill with sawdust pour melted wax over top. These are already waterproof. To use either of these fire starters set in the middle of the fire ring or grill stack up kindling around fire starter light the starter or the string. When kindling is burning good add more wood and enjoy your fire. Now back to the salad. Select a firm pineapple. To prepare, lay on side cut off both ends, using a sharp filet knife or serrated bread knife run down the side of the pineapple removing the skin. Do this all the way around the pineapple. The pineapple can be left whole cutting off round slices or cut in 1/2 long way remove core cut into half slices about 1/4 inch thick. Select honeydew and cantaloupe that are firm but not hard, cut of both ends set on end peel same as pineapple cut into 1/2 remove seeds. Cut slices lengthwise or across 1/4 inch at least. In a bowl or pan toss the pineapple, honeydew and cantaloupe with 1 c. of the pineapple cinnamon vinaigrette. Coat well. This can be done a day or 2 ahead just keep refrigerated until ready to use. When the wood has burned down into a nice bed of hot coals place the chicken on the grill when it is almost done add the pineapple and melon slices on the grill. If you want to marinade the chicken use something other than the pineapple cinnamon vinaigrette it will cause the chicken to burn really easy. I suggest using a mix of oil other than evoo with herbs marinade for 4-6 hrs. Grill the fruit to your liking the pineapple will tolerate more heat than the melons they will turn to mush if on the grill to long if the fire is really hot the melons will cook fast and mark beautiful. This salad looks really beautiful on a large dinner plate. Toss the baby greens in the pineapple cinnamon vinaigrette, place in the center of the dinner plates. Arrange the grilled fruits across baby greens add the berries and almonds. The almonds can be toasted the directions for this is in the recipe for Tye Pecan Chicken. Slice or dice the grilled chicken place on top of salad. More vinaigrette can be drizzled on the fruit and chicken. If you do not like almonds try pecans or cashews.

Pineapple Cinnamon Vinaigrette

2 c. pineapple (fresh or canned)
1/2 c rice wine vinegar
1 t. cinnamon
1 T. sugar or sugar substitute
1 c. canola, salad or vegetable oil
1/8 t. ks
1/4 c. fgbp

I prefer to use fresh pineapple but canned will work okay just drain well. Save the pineapple juice to make a cake or cupcakes. Peel the pineapple making sure to remove all the skin, cut into 1/2 inch or smaller pieces. Combine all the ingredients together; blend well using a kitchen blender or hand blender. For extra flavor add red chilies, jalapenos, habaneros, wasabi or even sesame oil.

Andy Bacon Berries & Arugula

6 c. Arugula
1 c. Bacon
1 c. Strawberries
1 c. Blue berries
1 c. Raspberries
12 ea. Grape or cherry tomatoes
1 c. Smoked cheddar cheese
1 c. Smoked ham
1 c. Smoked turkey
1 c. Smoked Bacon vinaigrette *(Simply Vinaigrettes)*

There is something about arugula that goes so well with smoked foods, lettuces and cabbages. Maybe it is because of the peppery taste arugula has. This salad is not for anyone who does not like smoked foods. To make this salad cook the bacon as crisp as you like save the grease for the vinaigrette or to cook popcorn in. Bacon grease to make popcorn? Oh yeah! It is the best. Drain the bacon well crumble to put in salad. In a large mixing bowl add the arugula, bacon, cut the strawberries in 1/2, 1/4 or slice. Add to the arugula, add the blue berries and raspberries. If you do not like either one of those berries add black berries or only strawberries. Cut the tomatoes in ½, slice or leave whole. The smoked cheddar cheese can be diced or shredded, more than one smoked cheese can be used such as smoked gouda, smoked mozzarella or smoked swiss cheese. Add the tomatoes and cheese to the arugula mix, next add the ham and turkey. Julienne cut or dice the ham and turkey. Usually with a salad containing meats and cheese I cut the cheese one way the meat another. Makes a nice contrast. Pour on the smoked bacon vinaigrette toss well. To serve this salad I like to use large dinner plates that are a bright color. In my recipe book *Janie's Simply Entrée Salads for Two*, I have a section in the back on plating. I am big on large plates and salad bowls with lots of solid colors. A bowl with a lot of designs distracts from the food. Ok back to plating this salad, after tossing everything together place in the center of large salad bowls, more crumbled bacon can be scattered across the top to garnish. If you do not want this salad tossed with the vinaigrette then mix everything together place in the bowls either drizzle with the vinaigrette or serve the vinaigrette on the side.

Smoke Bacon Vinaigrette

1/2 c. smoked bacon
2 t. garlic
1 c. cider vinegar
1 c. evoo or 1/2 c. bacon grease and 1/2 c evoo
1 c. canola, salad or vegetable oil
1 T. dijon mustard
1/2 t. crushed red chilies (optional)
1/2 t. ground cumin
1 t. fgbp

Replacing 1/2 the evoo with the bacon grease adds a lot more flavor I realized this after the recipe book was published. I learned a lot after *Simply Vinaigrettes* was published. For an Asian flair replace 1/2 the canola, salad or vegetable oil with sesame oil. There are other herbs that can be added for additional flavor such as fresh or dried ground ginger and fresh cilantro just to name a few. To make this vinaigrette, combine everything together in a container or blender; blend well. I do not add any more salt to this recipe but you can.

Nancy J. Yellow Roma Tomatoes & Bleu Cheese

6 c. Baby greens
14ea. Slices yellow roma tomato
1 c. Bleu cheese crumbles
1 c. Blue berries
1 c. Black raspberries
1 c. Almonds (toasted or candied)
1 c. Sheep cheese
1 c. Sweet Red Onion vinaigrette *(Simply Vinaigrettes)*
1/2 t. ks
1 t. fgbp

It is a shame that the season is so short for fresh home grown tomatoes. Yellow or orange roma tomatoes are really delicious. They are also called Italian tomatoes in some areas. I find yellow and orange tomatoes no matter what type to be sweeter than red tomatoes. People who have problems with red tomatoes can often eat the yellow and orange. This salad would be nice for a simple afternoon light lunch or early dinner. Maybe a bowl of soup and crusty bread before the salad! A grilled chicken breast can also be added. This is one of those salads that make a great dinner salad. Actually there are 3 ways to make this salad the quantities I have given above being the first the second and third are as follows quantities are for 2 servings.

2 c. baby greens	3 c. baby greens
3 slices yellow roma tomato	5 slices yellow roma tomato
1/4 c. blue cheese crumbles	1/2 c. blue cheese crumbles
1/4 c. blue berries	1/2 c. blue berries
1/4 c. black berries	1/2 c. black berries
1/4 c. almonds (toasted or untoasted)	1/2 c. almonds (toasted or untoasted)
1/4 c. sheep cheese	1/2 c. sheep cheese
1/4 c. Sweet Red Onion vinaigrette	1/2 c. Sweet Red Onion vinaigrette
1/4 t. ks	1/2 t. ks.
1/4 t. fgbp.	12 t. fgbp

The recipe to toast nuts is in the recipe for Tye Pecan Chicken and the recipe for making candied nuts is in the recipe for Grandma Ikie Thousand Island Chicken. All nuts are toasted and candied in the same way. The type of sheep cheese you use is your choice they come in soft or firm, smoked or plain. For this salad I suggest the soft type usually sold in a log at the store just cut off a piece crumble on salad. To plate this salad I prefer to use a large dinner plate or smaller salad plate depending on the size salad you are making. Slice the yellow roma tomato arrange around the outer edge of the plate sprinkle with the salt and pepper crumble the bleu cheese over the tomatoes, then drizzle some of the vinaigrette over this. In a mixing bowl add the baby greens, sheep cheese either diced or crumbled your preference, add the berries and almonds either toasted or candied sometimes I do not toast or candy the nuts I just go for the natural raw taste. Pour on the vinaigrette toss place on the plates in the center of the tomatoes making sure the tomatoes and bleu cheese are seen. Extra almonds, berries and cheese can be added on top. Just about any vinaigrette is great on this salad there are plenty to choose from between all my recipe books. The sweet red onion is my favorite for this salad.

Sweet Red Onion Vinaigrette

1/2 c. red onion
1/4 T. garlic
1 T. fresh or dried thyme
1 c. sherry vinegar
1 c. canola, salad or vegetable oil
1 c. evoo
1 c. sugar
1/2 t ks
1 t. fgbp

Peel the red onion cut into pieces place in a container or blender add the rest of the ingredients blend well. There are many other vinaigrettes that can be made from this one. Try adding 1 c. of canned sweet cherries or fresh cherries, peaches, jalapenos, habaneros, well you get the idea. It is such fun to play with vinaigrettes by adding different flavors.

Sue Festive Fruit

6 c. Baby greens
2 ea. Kiwi
1 ea. Mango
1 c. Dried cranberries
1 c. Black berries
1 c. Blue berries
1 c. Candied walnuts
1 c. Smoked Gouda cheese
1 c. Feta cheese
4 c. Chicken (white or dark)
1 c. Cranberry vinaigrette *(Simply Vinaigrettes* the recipe for this vinaigrette is in the recipe for Nancy B. Cranberry Cashew Chicken)

Festive salad? Oh Yeah! This is a very festive salad. Very colorful with the green kiwi, dried cranberries, blackberries, blueberries, greens and reds of the baby greens. Oh Yeah! The cheeses add a lot of flavor. The feta cheese is white and the smoked gouda is a light amber color. This is another great way to use leftover chicken again. The chicken you use for this salad is up to you grilled, baked, boiled, fried they will all work dice or shred the chicken place in a large mixing bowl. Peel dice or slice the kiwi, peel and dice the mango add them both to the chicken. Add the dried cranberries if you do not like cranberries there are a lot of other choices of dried fruit. Add the berries and candied walnuts to the chicken mix. The recipe for making candied nuts is in the recipe for Grandma Ikie Thousand Island Chicken as well as the recipe to make dried fruit. If you do not like nuts or have nut allergies in your family or friends try sunflower seeds or soybeans both add a lot to salads and can be candied. The smoked gouda cheese either dice or shred do not like smoked cheeses us plain gouda or do not like gouda try muenster or any other cheese. The feta can be crumbled or diced, again do not like feta cheese or goat cheese at all try swiss or white cheddar. Add the cranberry vinaigrette toss well, place in large salad bowls more candied walnuts can be put on top to garnish. Pork is also great for this salad. There are other vinaigrettes that work really well with this salad, blackberry thyme, strawberry rosemary, mandarin orange, these are also used in other recipes in this book also available in *(Simply Vinaigrettes)*. Chilies such as jalapeno, habanero, cayenne or what ever your choice is makes any vinaigrette and salad better.

Peach Tree Fruit Trio

1 ea. Fresh apricot
1 ea. Fresh peach
1 ea. Fresh plum
1 c. Sycamore slaw (recipe follows)
1 c. Tuna salad (recipe follows)
1 c. Chicken salad (recipe follows)
6 c. Baby greens
1 c. Strawberries
1 c. Blueberries
1 c. Candied pecans
1 c. Strawberry Rosemary Vinaigrette *(Simply Vinaigrettes)*

Tree fruit? Is this a new fruit no one knows about? No! it is the name I gave this salad because that is what apricots, peaches and plums are. They are also referred to as stone fruit because of the seed in them. These fruits can also be bought canned. I prefer to use fresh, unfortunately these fruits are not available year around at a reasonable price. If you choose to use canned drain them well. Do not discard the juices, they are great for replacing liquids in cakes, pancakes, waffles or cupcakes. Also for adding to water and teas. I have given several different recipes for tuna salad and chicken salad in my recipe book *"Janie's Simply Entrée Salads for Two."* I give another one in this recipe. The recipe for making candied nuts is in the recipe for Grandma Ikie Thousand Island Chicken. To serve this salad I use large dinner plates, start by tossing the baby greens in the strawberry rosemary vinaigrette place in the center of the plates. Place one 1/2 of each apricot, peach and plum on top of greens, place half the tuna salad, chicken salad and slaw in the center of each half fruit. Slice or cut the strawberries in 1/4 scatter over the plate along with the blueberries and candied pecans.

Tuna Salad

1 1/3 oz. can tuna
2 ea. stalks celery
3 ea. hard boiled eggs
1/4 c. white or red onion
1/4–1/2 c. 1000 island dressing (the recipe for this is in the recipe for Nate H. Macaroni Salad)
1 t. fgbp

Fresh tuna steaks grilled and flaked can be used in place of canned tuna. If using canned tuna drain well place in a mixing bowl, dice the celery, eggs, and onion. Add to tuna start with 1/4 c. of the 1000 island dressing mix well add more dressing if to dry. Make sure to add the pepper; a little salt can also be added. This is best if made 1-2 days ahead. Do not keep any unused more than 5 days.

Chicken Salad

8 oz. chicken (white or dark meat)
1/2 c. grapes
1/2 c almonds (toasted or untoasted recipe for toasting nuts is in the recipe for Tye Pecan Chicken)
2 ea. stalks celery
1/2-1 c. mayonnaise (homemade or processed recipe is in the recipe for Alicia Curried Chicken)
1 t. ks.
1 t. fgbp

This is another great way to use leftover chicken, dice or shred chicken place in a mixing bowl, cut grapes in 1/2 or 1/4 add to chicken, add the almonds, dice the celery add to chicken mix, add salt and pepper start with 1/2 c. mayonnaise mix well add more mayonnaise if to dry I would suggest start by adding 1 T. at a time. This chicken salad is better if made 1 or 2 days ahead. After 5 days, discard whatever is unused.

Sycamore Slaw

1 c. green cabbage
1 ea. red apple
1/2 c. red onion
1/4 c. pecans (untoasted)
1/2–1 c. poppy seed dressing (the recipe or this is in the recipe for Chris N. Cabbage with Apples)

Slice the cabbage very thin, dice the apples toss with 1/2 c. of the poppy seed dressing, fine dice the red onion add to cabbage and apples toss in the pecans mix well. This is also better if made 1-2 days ahead of time. Discard any that is unused after 7 days.

Strawberry Rosemary Vinaigrette

1 c. strawberries (fresh or frozen)
2 t. ground rosemary
1/2 c. rice wine vinegar
1/2 c. evoo
1/2 c. canola, salad or vegetable oil
1/4 c. sugar
1/4 t. ks
1/2 t. fgbp

If you are using frozen strawberries make sure they are the IQF (individual quick frozen) the frozen strawberries that are cooked frozen in juice do not work. The end result looks awful so use fresh or IQF. Put everything together; blend well.

Christy Crabby Dried Fruit

6 c. Baby greens
2 c. Crab meat (real or imitation)
1 c. Coconut (toasted)
1 c. Pecans (untoasted)
1/2 c. Dried cherries
1/2 c. Dried cranberries
1/2 c. Dried pineapple
1/2 c. Dried apricots
1 c. Coconut vinaigrette *(Simply Vinaigrette)*

This is one crabby salad that will put a smile on your face. The choice is yours real crabmeat or imitation crab meat. The fresh crab meat is the best of course. They both can be bought at most grocery stores in the fresh meat case or frozen. If you buy frozen thaw then use a paper towel or cloth towel to squeeze out the excess liquid. The dried fruits add a nice chewy sweet bite. Dried fruits can be bought at most food stores or you can make them yourself. The directions for making your own dried fruit are in the recipe for Grandma Ikie Thousand Island Chicken. All fruits dry the same way. The only dried fruit I do not find already diced or sliced is apricots they can be cut in 1/2 or 1/4. All the dried fruits can be mixed together then put in a zip lock bag for storage keep in a dry place. Just measure out what you need. There are a lot of uses for dried fruit, add to uncooked rice use apple juice for the liquid, try adding ginger, cinnamon or curry before cooking. Eat the rice by itself hot or cold also try adding chicken or pork before cooking. Now back to the salad. Dried fruit is also great added to popped corn plain or carmel. The directions for toasting coconut is in the recipe for Martin Very Berry Coconut Shrimp. I do not toast the pecans for this salad that does not mean you cannot toast it. Try toasting the pecans and coconut together. I like to use large salad bowls for this salad. To prepare this salad place the baby greens, crabmeat, dried fruits, toasted coconut, pecans and coconut vinaigrette in a mixing bowl toss everything together place in the center of the salad bowls garnish with more coconut and pecans. There are other vinaigrettes that are great for this salad, such as cranberry coconut, tequila lime ancho chili or lemon thyme just to mention a few. All these vinaigrettes are in my recipe book *Simply Vinaigrettes From Ancho Chili to White Wine.*

Coconut Vinaigrette

1/4 c. sugar
1/2 can coconut milk
3/4 c. rice wine vinegar
1 1/2 c. canola, salad or vegetable oil
1 1/2 c. evoo
1 t. tarragon (dried or fresh)
1/2 t. ks
1 t. fgbp

Shake the can of coconut milk really good open from the bottom scrap all the residue from the can lid do not miss any it is so awesome and sweet. Save the other 1/2 of the can to use for soup, sauce, pudding or as part of the liquid to make oatmeal. Combine all the ingredients together in a blender or container using a hand held blender; blend well. Refrigerate any unused portions but you may want to make extra it is so awesome for so many different foods.

Belinda Chipotle Peppers & Berries

2 c. Baby greens
2 c. Romaine lettuce
2 c. Nappa cabbage
1 c. Strawberries (fresh or frozen)
1 c. Blueberries (fresh or frozen)
1 c. Red raspberries (fresh or frozen)
1 c. Papaya (fresh, canned or dried)
1 c. Walnut halves (toasted or candied.
1 c. Goat cheese (soft)
1 ea. Red or green apple
1 ea. Pear
2 ea. 6 oz. Chicken breast
1 c. Herb marinade (*Janie's Simply Entrée Salads*)
1 c. Chipotle Peppers Vinaigrette *(Simply Vinaigrettes)*

Here I am again! Heat, sweet and cheese. Any of these can be added to any salad to liven it up. The heat comes from the chipotle peppers vinaigrette. The sweet is from all the fruits they are very sweet, especially if you use dried papaya it is dried with sugar. Fruit and chilies are great together. I actually suggest fresh or canned papaya. To use a fresh papaya the skin is actually eatable or can be peeled with a vegetable peeler. Cut the papaya in 1/2 remove the seeds which can be toasted like nuts and added to the salad, dice put in a mixing bowl, slice or cut the strawberries into 1/2 or 1/4 if you cannot find good fresh strawberries go to the freezer section get individual quick frozen strawberries called IQF they will work in a pinch do not buy the frozen that are cooked packed in there juice they are fine for strawberry shortcake not salads or vinaigrettes. Fresh or frozen blackberries and raspberries can be used also. I do not encourage the use of frozen berries but like I said in a pinch they will work. Put the papaya and berries with the strawberries, the apple and pear can be diced tossed with a small amount of lemon water to help slow down the browning or in some of the vinaigrette, if you use lemon water wait until the last minute drain well add to the berries toss gently, the walnuts can be toasted or candied for more crunch and sweetness the directions for toasting nuts is in the recipe for Tye Pecan Chicken and the candied nuts in the recipe for Grandma Ikie Thousand Island Chicken. The cheese! AH the cheese! Goat cheese goes so well with fresh fruits and lettuces. There are so many great cheeses to use if you do not like plain soft goat cheese, there is smoked gouda which is goat cheese, bleu cheese, muenster, cheddars that are mild, sharp and smoked. Actually a smoke cheese would go great with the chipotle pepper vinaigrette. The chicken can be marinated in some of the chipotle pepper vinaigrette or herb vinaigrette for 4-6 hours before grilling. Grilling is my favorite way to serve chicken on a salad. I am a believer that all meats, poultry, seafood, fish and pork are better if marinated before cooking. Lettuces, let's talk about them. Baby greens are fresh, crisp and colorful, romaine is hearty and crisp, and nappa cabbage is my favorite cabbage sweet and holds up well to vinaigrettes and dressings.

The baby greens are already picked, washed ready to go the romaine can be bought already cut into bite size pieces or you can buy a whole head cut it up yourself it is also available in packages of just the center leaves called hearts they are the sweetest tenderest. The nappa cabbage comes in heads like the romaine to cut start at the very end slice in thin slices across the head the leaves are very tender and sweet looking like lace. If you do not want slices of nappa make cuts the length of the head cut across in bite size pieces. Combine all the lettuces in a large mixing bowl add berries, papaya, apples, pears and walnuts, the cheese can be added now or spread over the top when plated. Add the chicken diced to the lettuce mix add the vinaigrette toss carefully so you do not smash the berries. To plate this salad, I like to use large dinner plates. Place the tossed salad in the center of plates if you have not added the cheese do so now more nuts can be added on top. This salad can also be served not tossed to do this mix the lettuces together place in the center of the plates add the fruits and berries, cheese, nuts and chicken drizzle with the vinaigrette or serve on the side. This salad is also great with seafood, fish, pork, or beef.

Herb Marinade

1 c. canola, salad or vegetable oil
1 t. garlic powder
1 t. fgbp
1 t. onion powder
1 t. dry oregano
1 t. cayenne pepper
1 t. dry basil

The quantities given are for a single use size. The amounts of the dry ingredients can be increased stored in a zip lock bag or container with a tight lid measured out when needed. To use, measure the oil and add the dry ingredients mix well add chicken let marinade for several days before use keep in the refrigerator. This marinade is great for anything seafood, fish, beef, or pork. Once you use it, your opinion will be "How have I done without this marinade for so long?" There is no vinegar or acid of any kind in this marinade, so whatever you marinate will be safe to use up to 7 days as long as you have kept it refrigerated. Discard after use.

Chipotle Peppers Vinaigrette

1 7oz. can chipotle peppers in adobo sauce
2 t. garlic
1 c. cider vinegar
1 c. canola, salad or vegetable oil
1 c. evoo
1/2 t. ks
1/2 t. fgbp

Chipotle chilies are a dried smoked jalapeno pepper that is reconstituted in a sauce called adobo. It is made of tomato paste, vinegar and garlic. Use the chilies as well as the adobo sauce. To make this vinaigrette, add everything together; blend well. If you are not sure how much jalapeno you can handle start out with 2 of the peppers and 1 T. of the sauce blend then adjust taste. The cider vinegar can be replaced with lemon juice or orange juice as the whole measurement or only 1/2. Sweet can also be added sweet and hot go hand in hand. If you do not use the whole can of chipotle place in a closed container in the fridge use for sauces and soups they will last about 2 weeks.

Gary Grilled Tuna with Sliced Fruit & Berries

6 c. Baby greens
4 ea. Slices pineapple
4 ea. Slices honeydew
4 ea. Slices cantaloupe
8 ea. Strawberries
1 c. Almonds (toasted)
2ea. 6 oz. Tuna steaks
1 c. Wasabi Vinaigrette (recipe follows)

Another salad with fruits and nuts? Why yes. Sweet melons and pineapples are so good with fresh grilled tuna or any fish or seafood. Another suggestion for this salad is smoked meats, sausages and brats. Summer is a great time for this salad when melons and berries are at their best. I suggest the almonds be toasted for extra crunch for this salad the directions for toasting nuts is in the recipe for Tye Pecan Chicken. When selecting a pineapple pick one that is firm not soft with dark green leaves. The honeydew and cantaloupe need to smell fresh and be firm also. If you have never peeled pineapple, honeydew or cantaloupe the directions to do this are in the recipe for Janie S. Fire Roasted Fruit & Chicken. After peeling the pineapple and melons slice 1/4 inch thick. The strawberries can be left whole or cut in 1/2. Use large dinner plates for this salad something black really makes the colors stand out. To plate place the baby greens in the center of the plate top each plate with 2 slices of each melon and pineapple add the strawberries and almonds. Slice the tuna steak place on each plate drizzle with the wasabi vinaigrette. this salad can also be plated tossed to do this place the greens in a large bowl, dice the pineapple, cantaloupe and honeydew add to bowl cut the strawberries into 1/4 add to greens mix along with the almonds dice the tuna steaks add to bowl pour on the vinaigrette toss carefully place in center of plates. More almonds can be added to top.

Wasabi Vinaigrette

The quantities I give are enough for this salad. After 2 days the heat of the wasabi is gone. The flavor or taste is still there but the kick is gone. Add more wasabi powder to bring it back.

3 T. wasabi powder or paste
2 t. garlic
1 T. soy sauce
1/2 c. rice wine vinegar
1 1/2 c. canola, salad or vegetable oil
1 t. sugar
1/4 t. ks
1/2 t. fgbp

Add everything together and blend well. There are other vinaigrettes that will be great on this salad. Such as pineapple vinaigrette, wasabi ginger sesame vinaigrette, Creole vinaigrette and ginger sesame vinaigrettes. These recipes are in my other recipe books *Simply Vinaigrettes from Ancho Chili to White Wine* and *Janie's Simply Entrée Salads for Two.*

Larry Asian Spinach, Arugula & Endive

2 c. Spinach
2 c. Arugula
2 c. Endive
1 c. Blueberries
1 c. Red raspberries
1 c. Mandarin oranges
1 c. Almonds (untoasted)
2 ea. 6oz. Chicken breast
8 ea. Wonton wrappers
1 c. Sesame Bacon Vinaigrette (recipe follows)

When the Asian craving in you kicks up but also the salad craving is kicking up this salad is perfect for you. Arugula is a large leaf herb with a peppery taste that is used like lettuce. Endive comes in a small bullet shaped head. This you need to slice into bite size pieces. Alone endive has a bitter taste combined with other lettuces and foods the bitterness is absorbed by other flavors. The spinach is good to go when purchased usually sometimes there may be some sand still on it just wash in clean cold water pat or spin dry. I use blueberries and red raspberries because the colors and flavors go so well with the spinach, arugula and endive. If you are lucky to find fresh mandarin oranges use them defiantly. They can be bought in cans and jars in this wonderful juice. Do not toss it out. Drink it, add to cakes, teas, pancakes, waffles and juices. The almonds I leave untoasted it just tastes right. Wonton wrappers are found in the produce section of most stores. These I leave whole drop in hot oil fry crisp. You can cut into strips if you choose. They fry really fast so watch they do not burn do not let your oil get hot enough to smoke. To serve this salad I like to use 2 large salad bowls. To make this salad start with a large mixing bowl add all the spinach, arugula and endive, add the berries, mandarin oranges and almonds, toss with the sesame bacon vinaigrette. Slice or dice the chicken place on top of salads, place wontons 4 on each salad on the sides. If using strips, spread over the salad. Sesame seeds can be added on top they toast just like nuts. The directions for toasting sesame seeds is in the recipe for Marcella Oriental Beef. The chicken can be marinated in sesame oil before grilling for extra flavor.

Sesame Bacon Vinaigrette

1/4 c. bacon
1 t. garlic
1/2 c. rice wine vinegar
1/4 c. evoo
1/4 c. bacon grease
1/4 c. canola, salad or vegetable oil
1/4 c. sesame oil
1 t. fgbp

Cook the bacon crisp remove from pan reserve grease for vinaigrette if there is not enough to make 1/4 c. use canola, salad or vegetable oil to make up the difference. Do not use sesame oil to make the difference unless you want a strong sesame taste. Sesame is wonderful, but too much is not. I do not add any more salt there is plenty in the vinaigrette between the bacon and grease. To make this vinaigrette put everything together in a container blend well with a hand blender or use an electric blender. Crushed red chilies, jalapenos or wasabi can be added for extra kick.

Rick Fresh Fruit & Nuts

2 c. Iceberg lettuce
2 c. Spinach
2 c. Romaine lettuce
1 ea. Apple
1 ea. Pear
2 ea. Fresh oranges
1/4 Pineapple
1/4 Honeydew
1/4 Cantaloupe
1 c. Strawberries
1 c. Red raspberries
1 c. Almonds (toasted or untoasted)
1 c. Pistachios (toasted or untoasted)
2 ea. 6oz. Chicken breasts or Tuna steaks
2 c. Sweet Italian Vinaigrette *(Janie's Simply Entrée)*

There is nothing more refreshing in the summer time than a salad of fresh fruits, berries and nuts. This is the perfect time of year for lots of fresh fruits and berries. Other fruits that are plentiful this time of year are plums, peaches, figs and apricots just to mention a few, there are also other berries like black berries and boysenberries. All of these can be added or used in place of the fruits in this recipe. Let's not forget all the varieties of grapes. Make the vinaigrette a few days before using to really get the full flavor of it. I suggest marinating the chicken or tuna in some of the sweet Italian vinaigrette 4-6 hrs. before cooking. Start preparing this salad by dicing the apple, pear and oranges toss all 3 together with a small amount of the vinaigrette in a large mixing bowl. Peel pineapple, honeydew and cantaloupe, you are using only 1/4 of each for this salad dice add to the apple mix. If you are not sure how to peel these 3 fruits the directions for this are in the recipe for Janie S. Fire Roasted Fruit & Chicken. Slice or quarter the strawberries add the other fruit mix, save the red raspberries to put on top. The nuts can be toasted or untoasted the choice is yours if you want to toast them the recipe for this is in the recipe for Tye Pecan Chicken. Either way you use them add to the fruit mix, make sure you gently toss all this together so you do not bruise or smash any of the fruit. By the way bananas are great added to this salad. The lettuces, why all three? Iceberg I decided to add because and I do not know why but a lot of people love it even though it has no nutritional value at all it is mostly water, the spinach I add for flavor and is very good for you a great source of iron, the romaine is very hearty adds a nice crunch. I am not an expert in what is good for you vitamin and mineral wise I just know what tastes good. Mix these 3 together. This salad looks great on large dinner plates or large salad bowls. Whichever you choose place 1/2 the lettuce mix in the center top with the fruit, berries and nuts mix, slice the chicken or tuna steaks place on top of each plate add the red raspberries drizzle with the vinaigrette. This salad is also great with all the ingredients including the raspberries and vinaigrette tossed together then place in the bowls or on the plates. The chicken or tuna can be left off for a great vegetarian salad; it is also a great crowd pleaser for a buffet. Double the recipe for a buffet salad to feed between 6-8 people.

Sweet Italian Vinaigrette

1/2 c. sugar or sugar substitute
1 c. rice wine vinegar
1 c. evoo
1 T. Italian seasoning
1/8 t. ks
1/2 t. fgbp

This is one of those vinaigrettes that are great made with a sugar substitute especially in a salad full of fruits and berries. Italian seasoning is found in the spice section of any food store. If you prefer to blend your own that is even better. This is one of those vinaigrettes that are fast to make I just put everything together in a bowl and use a wire whip to blend. Crushed red chilies or cayenne pepper can be added for extra zip. Yes I like extra zip, chilies are your friends you do not need to be afraid of them when used in the right way.

Chris K. Pineapple, Spinach, & Smoked Ham

3 c. Spinach
3 c. Arugula
1/4 Cantaloupe
1/4 Honeydew
1/4 Pineapple
1 c. Grapes (red or green)
1 ea. Pear
1 c. Blackberries
1 c. Strawberries
1 c. Dill Havarti cheese
1 c. Feta cheese
2 c. Smoked ham
1 c. Walnuts (toasted halves or pieces)
1 c. Pear Vinaigrette *(Janie's Simply Entrée)*

Arugula and spinach together again? Yes! They go so well together like peanut butter and jelly. They also blend very well with all kinds of fruits, berries and nuts. If you do not like arugula use all spinach or 1/2 spinach 1/2 baby greens or cabbage, if you like arugula but not spinach use baby greens or cabbage. This salad is a great way to use leftover fruits and berries. Once a melon of any variety has been peeled and cut into it will last about 4 days in the fridge of course they can be cut up and frozen to use in salads or for chilled soups.

I love a bowl of frozen fruits made with melons and berries but watch out for the brain freeze try adding some vanilla ice cream or a sherbet. Do not forget the chocolate sauce. Now on to the salad. Place the spinach and arugula in a large mixing bowl; this is one of those salads that everything goes in to the pool. Dice the cantaloupe, honeydew and pineapple the directions for peeling these are in the recipe for Janie S. Fire Roasted Fruit & Chicken, add to the spinach and arugula, cut the grapes in 1/2 or 1/4 add to bowl, add the blackberries, cut the strawberries into 1/2 or slice, dice the pear add to the rest, shred or dice the dill havarti cheese, dice or crumble the feta cheese add these to the party mix, I like to either thin slice then julienne cut (cut in strips) or dice the ham, the walnuts I like to toast to really bring out the walnut taste the directions for toasting nuts is in the recipe for Tye Pecan Chicken. Add the pear vinaigrette toss well serve in large pasta or salad bowls. The pear can be sliced instead of diced and placed on top of the salad to be drizzled with more pear vinaigrette and more walnuts can be sprinkled on top. There are many other smoked meats that can be used in place of or with the ham such as turkey, pork, or chicken.

Pear Vinaigrette

2 ea. pears
1 T. thyme (fresh, frozen or dried)
1/2 c. cider vinegar
1/2 c. canola, salad or vegetable oil
1/2 c. evoo
1/4 t. ks
1/4 t. fgbp.
1-2 T. sugar

The pears do not need to be peeled the skin blends fine if you cannot stand skin on anything like fruits and vegetable then peel them. Canned pears can also be used just drain well. I have found that canned fruits work just fine for vinaigrettes but must be drained well or your vinaigrette will be very thin. Cut the pears in 1/2 remove the seeds, core(cut out that center stringy stuff & seeds), cut into 4 pieces combine everything together in a container for a hand blender or electric blender using 1 T. of sugar to start blend everything together, taste for tart ness add more sugar if needed. You can always add more but you cannot take it away. If you do not like thyme try adding basil or cinnamon. Rosemary or tarragon tends to take over the taste. This is one of those vinaigrettes that is great mixed 1/2 and 1/2 with vinaigrette such as pineapple, raspberry, jalapeno or even cayenne.

Matt H. Peanuts, Berries, Cheese, & Chipotle

6 c. Baby greens
1 c. Strawberries
1 c. Cheddar cheese
1 c. Peanuts
1 c. Dried blueberries (the directions for making your own dried fruit are in the recipe for Grandma Ikie Thousand Island Chicken)
1 c. Dried pineapple
2 ea. 6 oz. Chicken breasts
1 c. Chipotle Peanut Sesame vinaigrette (recipe follows)

Chipotle peppers again? Does this chef & author have a thing for chipotle peppers? Why yes I do! Also habaneros, serrano's, jalapenos and any other hot peppers there are. I explain about them in the recipe for Belinda Chipotle Peppers & Berries. The combination of the fresh strawberries and dried fruits with the chipotle peanut sesame vinaigrettes is well there are not words to describe the sensation. The crunch of the baby greens and peanuts with the firmness of the cheddar cheese is really pleasing. Other cheeses can be used along with or instead of the cheddar cheese such as pepper jack or Monterey jack cheese. To make this salad start by placing the baby greens in a large mixing bowl add the strawberries cut in 1/2 or 1/4, the cheddar cheese can be diced or shredded, add to the baby greens, toast the peanuts it really improves the crunch and taste, the directions for toasting nuts is in the recipe for Tye Pecan Chicken, add to the other ingredients, next add the dried blueberries and dried pineapple, the chicken can be fresh cooked or leftover I like to dice, or shred the chicken put in the bowl with rest of the ingredients add the vinaigrette toss everything well. Place in the center of large dinner plates more toasted peanuts can be added to garnish. Toasted sesame seeds can be added tossed in or on top of the salad. Sesame seeds toast the same way as nuts do.

Chipotle Peanut Sesame Vinaigrette

1 c. rice wine vinegar
1 c. peanut butter
1 c. toasted peanuts
1/2 c. sugar
1/2 c. canola, salad or vegetable oil
1/2 c. sesame oil
1-2 ea. chipotle chilies
3 T. soy sauce
1 1/2 t. ginger
2 t. garlic

This vinaigrette takes a little longer to blend. If you have ever made homemade peanut butter you know what I mean. The peanuts will not completely blend. This vinaigrette will have the texture of creamy with sand, but fear not for the taste is great and unlike sand the peanuts do chew well. Toast the peanuts it deepens the taste. Peel and cut the ginger into small pieces. It will string not chop well if you do not. Start with 1 chipotle chili then blend and taste. If the heat is too mild, add another chipotle pepper and blend again. Simply add all the ingredients together; blend well.

Dougie Mandarin Orange

4 c. Baby greens

2 c. Romaine

2 c. Mandarin oranges

1 c. Bacon

12 ea. Cherry tomatoes

1 c. Almonds (toasted or untoasted the directions for toasting nuts is in the recipe for Tye Pecan Chicken)

1 c. Dried cherries (the recipe for making dried fruit is in the recipe for Grandma Ikie Thousand Island Chicken)

1 c. Mandarin Orange Vinaigrette *(Janie's Simply Entrée)*

8 ea. Breaded chicken tenders

Dried fruit again? Yes I love dried fruit. Sweet, chewy, such intense fruit taste. If you have to watch your sugar intake take it easy on the dried fruit. Most of them are coated in sugar or honey when processed, the best way for us who have to watch our sugars is to make our own dried fruits. The combination of the baby greens (sweet and tender) with the heartier romaine lettuce makes for a nice bite. The smoky bacon complements the dried fruit and cherry tomatoes. The almonds add a nice crunch. Toasted or untoasted is your choice. The mandarin oranges add a nice sweet orange taste. Mandarin oranges and almonds are great together. To make your own breaded chicken tenders, start with either already cut chicken tenders or cut whole chicken breasts into 6-8 pieces. Set up a breading station. To do this use shallow bowls or pie pans, the first bowl have flour seasoned with salt, pepper and garlic if you choose. The 2nd bowl beat 2 whole eggs with 1 T. water; in the 3rd bowl add seasoned bread crumbs, crushed cornflakes or the breading of your choice which could be flour again. Coat the chicken tenders with flour then coat with the egg wash then into the 3rd breading. Have oil for frying the chicken tenders ready when you are done breading them. They can be breaded a day ahead kept in the fridge until ready to fry. Oven baked is also a choice. Cook until golden brown and done. The grease from the bacon can also be used to cook the chicken tenders. To make this salad use a large mixing bowl add the baby greens, and romaine, mandarin oranges, crumble or chop the bacon add to the mix, cut the cherry tomatoes in 1/2 or 1/4 add to bowl next add the almonds and dried cherries then pour on the vinaigrette toss really well. Place in the center of 2 large dinner plates. Cut the chicken tenders into 3 pieces each place on top of the salad more vinaigrette can be drizzled on top of the chicken. This salad can also be plated without tossing. Put the lettuces in the center of the large dinner plates add the mandarin oranges, bacon, cherry tomatoes, almonds and dried cherries top with the chicken tenders serve the dressing on the side or drizzle over the salad. The chicken tenders can also be tossed in with the rest of the salad.

Mandarin Orange Vinaigrette

2 c. mandarin oranges with juice
1 c. rice wine vinegar
2 c. canola, salad or vegetable oil
1 t. thyme (fresh, dried or frozen)
1/8 t. ks
1/4 t. fgbp

You notice I say mandarin oranges and juice yes the juice has lots of flavor, combine everything together; blend well. Crushed red chilies or cayenne pepper can be added for zing.

Rich Mango Ginger

6 c. Baby greens
1 c. Mango ginger cheese
1 c. Almonds (untoasted)
1 c. Dried mango (the recipe to dry fruit is in the recipe for Grandma Ikie Thousand Island Chicken)
1 c. Green onions or chives
2 ea. 6 oz. Chicken breasts
1 c. Thai Coconut vinaigrette (recipe follows)
1 c. Coconut (toasted the recipe for this is in the recipe for Martin Very Berry Coconut Shrimp)

Are you ready for a taste of Thai? How about a taste of mango? Here they are, together in a salad. For a more authentic Thai flair use nappa or green cabbage instead of or with the baby greens. I am constantly amazed at all the varieties of cheeses there are. I will never in my lifetime as much as I would like to get a chance to sample every cheese there is, domestic and imported. Mango ginger cheese is one I am glad I got to try. The cheese itself has a creamy tart taste. The texture is crumbly full of dried crystallized ginger and dried mango. What is crystallized ginger? It is fresh ginger usually diced cooked in sugar water simmered until all the liquid is evaporated with nothing left but pieces of candied ginger. Candied ginger I thought it was crystallized ginger to me it is the same thing when all the water evaporates from sugar water sugar crystals is what you have left. When it comes to nuts I usually suggest they be toasted or candied not in this case. I do recommend sliced or slivered almonds. Cashews will work great also. More dried mango? There is some already in the cheese! Yes but more only intensifies the mango taste. Green onions add the right amount of onion taste. Use the whole onion or chive chop from end to end. No matter how you cook the chicken, bake, grill or roast marinade in the Thai coconut vinaigrette for 4-6 hours before cooking. I like to serve this salad in large salad bowls. In a large mixing bowl combine the baby greens, almonds, dried mango, green onions and coconut with the Thai coconut vinaigrette toss well place in the salad bowls thin slice the chicken place on top of the salad some green onions or chives can be scattered on the top. More vinaigrette can be drizzled over the chicken. Pork loin is also very nice served on this salad.

Thai Coconut Vinaigrette

1 can coconut milk
1/4 c. lemon grass
1/4 c. fresh ginger
2 c. rice wine vinegar
3 c. canola, salad or vegetable oil
1 c. evoo
1 t. ks
1 t. fgbp
1 c. coconut
1 t. sambol (Chinese chili)

This vinaigrette requires a little prep time, not too much just a little. To start shake the can of coconut milk open from the bottom. Most of the time the solids settle in the bottom. Shaking loosens it. If there is still solids on the lid scrape it off. You will want every bit of the coconut flavor. The lemon grass can be bought at any Asian market. It comes in hard stalks. Lay the stalk on a cutting board pound with a mallet or rolling pin to break up the fibers. It can now be chopped with a knife into small pieces that will blend without stringing. The fresh ginger can be bought at any food store. Peel with a paring knife or vegetable peeler, cut into very small pieces so it will not string but will blend well. The coconut can be fresh or processed but not toasted. Combine everything together either in a blender or a container using a hand blender. The longer you blend this vinaigrette the more lemon grass and ginger flavors come out. This vinaigrette is one of those that only gets better over time. Keep refrigerated the oils may harden with the coconut milk let set out for about 30 minutes give a stir good to go. If you cannot find sambol use crushed red chilies or a chili of your choice.

Charlotte Ginger Carrot

3 c. Nappa cabbage

3 c. Spinach

12 ea. Grape tomatoes

1 c. Bacon

1 c. Pineapple (grilled the directions for how to peel pineapple and grill are in the recipe for Janie S. Fire Roasted Fruit & Chicken)

1 c. Bean sprouts

1/2 Red bell peppers (roasted the directions for this is in the recipe for Linda M. Pasta Salad Tossed in Sweet Tomato Vinaigrette)

2 ea. 6 oz. Chicken breast, pork loin, tuna steaks, shrimp or salmon

1 c. Ginger Carrot Vinaigrette

This is one of those salads that has many layers of tastes and textures. Every bite will be an adventure. I chose the nappa cabbage and spinach for their flavors and textures. Nappa cabbage has a crisp crunch with a lacy look where the spinach adds bright green color with a firm bite. The grape tomatoes and pineapple add sweetness. The pineapple would really be great tossed in some of the ginger carrot vinaigrette then grilled or oven roasted. The bean sprouts add extra crunch. The best place to purchase bean sprouts is at an Asian market. The bell peppers can be roasted fresh by you or bought already done in a jar at any food store. The smoky bacon really rounds this salad out. I cannot decide what would go better on this salad so I decided everything except beef. Besides what I mentioned in the ingredients list there is also red snapper, seafood, clams, lobster, crab meat or even oysters. To assemble this salad pick a bright colored plate such as yellow or orange. Cut the nappa cabbage either into bite size pieces or slices toss with the spinach and bean sprouts place on the dinner plates, cut the grape tomatoes in 1/2 or 1/4 scatter over the plate, crumble the bacon over the salad, dice the pineapple over the salad unless you want to leave it in rings or slices, dice or julienne cut the roasted red bell peppers, slice the chicken, pork loin, tuna steaks, etc. or if using shrimp, clams, crab meat etc. place on top of the salad drizzle with the vinaigrette. This salad can also be tossed everything together with the vinaigrette then place on the plates. Sesame seeds can be scattered over the salad.

Ginger Carrot Vinaigrette

2 c. carrots
4 T. ginger
1 T. garlic
1 1/2 c. canola, salad or vegetable oil
1/2 c. evoo
1 c. rice wine vinegar
1 T. sugar
1 T. dijon mustard
1/2 t. ks
1/2 t. fgbp

The name of this vinaigrette says it all. The fresh crisp taste of the ginger and the sweetness of the carrots will make you smile. When purchasing the fresh ginger make sure the pieces are not dry. Peel the ginger with a paring knife cut into small pieces. The ginger can be grated using a small cheese grater. If you do it this way make sure you grate it over the container you are going to blend it in so you do not lose any of the wonderful juice. The carrots need to be peeled. They can be cut into small pieces or shredded to be blended. This vinaigrette will require some extra blending; carrots and ginger require more. Combine all the ingredients together in an electric blender or container for using a hand blender. This vinaigrette is also great on a grilled chicken or tuna steak sandwich. A small amount of horseradish can also be added to this vinaigrette fresh of course just add about 1 t. to start.

Mam Vegetarian Fruit

6 c. Baby greens
1/2 c. Almonds (toasted the recipe for this is in the recipe for Tye Pecan Chicken)
1/2 c. Peanuts (toasted)
1 ea. Pear
1 ea. Apple (red or green)
2 ea. Oranges
1 c. Strawberries
1 c. Blueberries
1 c. Red raspberries
1 c. Black berries
1 ea. Banana
1 c. Grapes (red, green or both)
1 ea. Peach
1 c. Grape Chipotle Vinaigrettes (recipe follows)

It is in the middle of summer, the girls are coming over for lunch by the pool. What would be better than a vegetarian fruit salad with chilled fruity flavored wine punch? Berries, pears, peaches and grapes are at their best. There are several ways to serve this salad. Whichever way you choose start by toasting the almonds and peanuts. To plate this salad with everything tossed together start by selecting either large dinner plates or large salad bowls. In a large mixing bowl place the baby greens, nuts, strawberries slice or quarter them first, add the other berries, peel the oranges then either dice up or cut out the sections between the membranes when done this way they are called supremes. Put in a separate mixing bowl dice the pear and apple, peel slice the banana toss with the oranges this will help stop them from turning brown as fast after tossing them together add to the baby greens mix, cut the grapes in 1/2 add to the rest of the mix, pour on the vinaigrette toss carefully so you do not smash the banana or berries. Place in the center of the large plates or bowls, sprinkle with more nuts. Another way is to use the large dinner plates or bowls add the baby greens then layer on the rest of the ingredients either drizzle with the grape chipotle vinaigrette or serve on the side. Still another option is toss everything together in a large mixing bowl with the vinaigrette serve in a large serving bowl. There is also the salad bar option place everything in separate bowls let everyone make their own. Fruit muffins or breads can be added with honey whipped butter or chipotle honey butter (recipe follows).

Grape Chipotle Vinaigrette

1 c. grape jelly (regular or sugar free)

2-3 ea. chipotle chilies (for information on what chipotle chilies are, I explain them in the recipe for Belinda Chipotle Peppers & Berries)

1 c. canola, salad or vegetable oil

1 c. evoo

1 t. garlic

1/4 t. ks

1/2 t. fgbp

1 c. rice wine vinegar

Yes you can use sugar free grape jelly. If you do not like grape, try blackberry jam or jelly—even apricot—but never strawberry jam (it does not work). As for the chipotle chilies my suggestion is to start with 2 add the rest of the ingredients blend well taste for the chipotle flavor add more 1 at a time. You can always add more but you cannot take away. Cilantro or tarragon can also be added for extra taste. Try this vinaigrette as a glaze for grilled chicken, pork or salmon. Brush it on after you have turned the grilled food over it will burn if you brush it on the top side then flip. It also makes a great dip for chicken wings, breaded chicken tenders or even breaded tenderloin sandwiches.

Mitzi Raspberry Papaya Salmon

6 c. Baby greens
2 c. Raspberries
1 c. Coconut (untoasted)
2 c. Cashews (untoasted)
1 ea. Papaya (directions for peeling the papaya and toasting the seeds are in the recipe for Pat P. A Blast Of Fruit)
1/4 c, Dijon mustard
2 ea. 6oz. Salmon steaks
1 c. Raspberry Vinaigrette *(Simply Vinaigrettes)*

How do I describe this salad? Sweet, nutty, fruity, fresh, crunchy and delicious. How is that for a description. To prepare the salmon spray a baking sheet preheat oven to 400 degrees, place the salmon on the baking sheet, spread with the dijon mustard, fine chop 1/2 of the cashews coat the mustard topped salmon with the cashews bake in the oven for 15-20 minutes until done add some liquid of some sorts white wine, apple juice or chicken stock works well not a lot maybe 1/4 c this keeps the salmon moist during baking. While the salmon is baking prepare the rest of the salad. In a large mixing bowl add the baby greens, raspberries, coconut, and 1/2 the cashews and the papaya. Toss with the raspberry vinaigrette and place in the center of 2 large dinner plates. Top with the salmon drizzle. More cashews can be sprinkled on top of the salmon. To serve this salad not tossed place the baby greens in the center of 2 large dinner plates add the rest of the ingredients top with the salmon serve the raspberry vinaigrette on the side or drizzle over the salad. If you do not like salmon at all, try using chicken, pork, tuna or shrimp. There are plenty of other nuts that are great also if you do not like cashews try pistachios or almonds.

Raspberry Vinaigrette

1 c. raspberry or rice wine vinegar
1 1/2 c. raspberries (fresh or frozen)
1 c. sugar
1 c. canola, salad or vegetable oil
1 c. evoo
1 T. thyme
1 T. oregano
1 T. basil
1 T. dijon mustard
1 t. ks
1 t. fgbp

Raspberry preserves can also be used for this vinaigrette. What preserves? Yes they are great for vinaigrettes right amount of sweet usually. But! There is always a but. Strawberry does not work it makes a runny vinaigrette that does not look appetizing. Apricot, pear, peach even plum work great use equal amount of preserves to replace the fresh fruit. If you cannot find raspberry vinegar try rice wine vinegar instead or go to a specialty store with flavor infused balsamic vinegars use that instead. Put all the ingredients together; blend well enjoy. This vinaigrette is also great brushed on grilled chicken, fish or pork. Use as a dipping sauce for the grilled meat also.

Stan Pineapple B.L.T.

3 c. Baby greens
3 c. Spinach
2 c. Bacon
2 ea. Roma tomatoes
1 c. Shredded parmesan cheese
2 c. Pineapple
2 ea. 6oz Chicken breast or 8 breaded chicken tenders
    (the directions for making your own chicken tenders
    is in the recipe for Dougie Mandarin Orange)
1 c. Pineapple Vinaigrette *(Janie's Simply Entrée)*
Spicy chicken marinade (recipe follows)

Pineapple and bacon again? What is wrong with this lady? Nothing I hope, I just like pineapple and bacon together it is like bologna and cheese. This gives me an idea for a sandwich pineapple, bacon, bologna and cheese on grilled rye. Try it let me know. I never get tired of baby greens and spinach together I hope you do not either. I like to cook the bacon crispy also I like to use thick sliced bacon or buy a slab slice it yourself. Save the bacon grease to use for vinaigrette or to make popcorn in. I chose roma tomatoes because they are sweet and meaty, cut in 1/2 remove seeds dice in bite size papers. The parmesan cheese can be shaved, shredded or chunked, the pineapple is peeled and diced. If you have never used a fresh pineapple the directions for peeling a fresh pineapple are in the recipe for Janie

S. Fire Roasted Fruit & Chicken. If you get more than 2 c. of pineapple from this use the rest for the vinaigrette. The chicken either whole breast or tenders can be marinated in my spicy chicken marinade kept in the fridge until used. I like to toss this salad as with most of my recipes then serve on 2 large dinner plates or in 2 large salad bowls. In a large mixing bowl add the baby greens, crumble the bacon, add diced romas and parmesan cheese toss well with the pineapple vinaigrette, place on the plates or in the bowls add the chicken breasts sliced on top if using chicken tenders leave them whole or cut in 2-3 pieces place on top of salad drizzle with more vinaigrette. Nuts or berries can be added to this salad for extra flavor and crunch.

Spicy Chicken Marinade

1 c. canola, salad or vegetable oil
1 t. garlic
1 t. cayenne pepper
1 t. fgbp
1/4 t. ks

Chop the garlic just a little, mix everything together well. If 1 t. is not enough cayenne for you try adding more 1/4 t. at a time. If you do not like cayenne pepper use crushed red chilies or jalapenos instead. Onion powder or fresh onion can also be added. The chicken breasts or chicken tenders can both be marinated. A zip lock bag is great for mixing and storing meat that is marinated.

There is no vinegar or acid in the marinade so the chicken can be marinated even 4-5 days before use. Be sure to discard the marinade after removing the chicken.

Pineapple Vinaigrette

1 c. pineapple (fresh or canned)
1/2 c. rice wine vinegar
1/2 c. evoo
1/2 c. canola, salad or vegetable oil
1/8 t. ks
1/4 t. fgbp

If you use canned pineapple make sure to drain it well. Keep the juice use it for marinades, sauces, mix with other juices, teas, in cakes you get the idea. If the pineapple is not diced do so, put all the ingredients together; blend well. You will have a lot of fun finding ways to use this vinaigrette other than as a vinaigrette for this salad. Sugar or artificial sweetener can be added if it is to tart for you. Start with 1/2 t. blend taste. For extra kick if you have an open can of chipotle peppers in the fridge try adding about 1/2 t. of the adobo sauce.

Bob Chicken & Fresh Mozzarella Pasta

6 c. Pasta

3 c. Chicken

2 c. Fresh mozzarella cheese

1 c. Pine nuts (toasted the recipe for this is in the recipe for Tye Pecan Chicken)

1 c. Black olives

2 c. Tomato Chive Roasted Garlic Vinaigrette (recipe follows)

The vinaigrette is what really makes this salad. The pasta you use is your choice. I have a few suggestions, cheese tortellini, spaghetti, angel hair, rotini or bowtie are my favorites. This salad is also a great way to use leftover pasta. If you use leftover pasta it should be reheated to do this, bring water to a boil put the pasta in it for 1-2 minutes drain well toss with the vinaigrette mixing well this makes for a more flavorful pasta the vinaigrette really soaks in. This also cools down the pasta. Some vinaigrettes do not hold up to putting on hot pasta or potatoes they break down this one does not. This salad is also a great way to use leftover chicken no matter how it is cooked. The vinaigrette is also much better when it is made up to a week ahead so the flavors can blend together or (marry) as the term is. To make this salad first decide what pasta you are using, cook until done toss with the vinaigrette, decide how the chicken is to be cooked, leftover, baked, roasted, grilled, boiled those roasted chickens from the grocery are good for this. Buy one for tonight's dinner use the rest for tomorrow's lunch or dinner. Dice or shred the chicken, add to the pasta, fresh mozzarella cheese is sold in grocery stores usually in a plastic bag with water. It is in balls or logs, smoked or plain. The smoked is not packed in water. Dice the fresh mozzarella add to the pasta and chicken. If you do not use all the fresh mozzarella cheese put in a container covered with water in the fridge to use for other salads, pizza, sandwiches you get the idea. This cheese will keep for 2 weeks in the fridge just change the water every day. Pine nuts are easy to find at grocery stores it is usually in the produce section they should be kept refrigerated they spoil easy. In fact all nuts can go rancid easily especially if toasted. Pine nuts toast just like nuts. They are exactly what their name is the nut of pine cones. They taste like pine not one of my favorite flavors. The small size are not as bitter as the large. Toasting pine nuts add a whole new level of flavor. After toasting let cool then add to the pasta mix. Store the leftover in a zip lock bag in the fridge or freezer. The black olives can be cut in 1/2 or sliced, other olives can also be used along with the black olives or in place of. Add to the pasta mix, pour on the vinaigrette toss well. This is one salad that really looks great served in a large pasta bowls especially if they are black. Shredded or grated parmesan cheese can be sprinkled over the top. Pork or seafood can also be used for this salad and of course the usual chilies I suggest can be added for extra flavor.

Tomato Chive Roasted Garlic Vinaigrette

2 c. diced tomatoes (canned or fresh)
1/2 c. dried chives
4 T. roasted garlic (the recipe for this is in the recipe for Randy Chicken with Pasta in Curry Roast Garlic Vinaigrette)
1 c. cider vinegar
1 c. canola, salad or vegetable oil
1 t. sugar
1/2 t. ks
1 t. fgbp

This is one of those vinaigrettes that get better the longer they set. Canned diced tomatoes in water or juice are easy to use for this vinaigrette. Drain them well save the juice or water from the canned to use in sauces, stocks, or even drinks. To use fresh tomatoes I suggest that you blanch them first to remove the skin. To do this first select fresh not overripe tomatoes, they do not have to be red, orange and or yellow can also be used. Bring a large pot of water to boil, have a bowl of ice water close by to chill down and help remove the skin. Wash the tomatoes remove the cores put a small x in the skin at the opposite end of the tomato. Place the tomatoes in the boiling water for no more than 2 minutes the skin should start to pull away from where the core was cut out and the other end with the x. carefully remove from the boiling water place in the ice water immediately the skin should almost peel off by itself. Remove from the ice water peel off the rest of the skin, cut in half remove the seeds dice. Place the diced tomatoes in a mixing bowl while you are blanching the tomatoes roast the garlic. After the garlic has roasted and cooled so it can be handled chop into small pieces do not puree you want the small pieces, garlic when roasted takes on a sweet taste. Add the roasted garlic to the tomatoes, add the dried chives. The reason I use dried chives is because the fresh do not hold up if you are using all the vinaigrette within a few months fresh are good to use. After about 2-3 months the fresh chives turn brown and do affect the flavor of the vinaigrette. Add the sugar, vinegar, oils, salt and pepper mix well with a spoon or wire whip. Balsamic vinegar can be used instead of cider vinegar for a whole new level of flavor and sweetness.

Tammy Heirloom Tomato

6 c. Baby greens
1 c. Goat cheese
2 c. Heirloom tomatoes
1 c. Dried cherries (the directions for making these yourself is in the recipe for Grandma Ikie Thousand Island Chicken)
12 ea. Sun gold or red cherry tomatoes
1 c. Bacon
1 c. Red onion
2 ea. 6oz. Chicken breast
1 c. Toasted Cumin Seed Vinaigrette *(Simply Vinaigrettes)*

Heirloom tomatoes—what is that? Heirloom tomatoes are not hybrid. That means they are grown from seeds that for generations have remained pure, not crossed with any other breeds of tomatoes. Heirloom tomatoes come in all sizes, colors, and shapes. There are some that are striped and beautiful. This is the one I like to use. Heirloom tomatoes may be hard to find in some areas. They are almost impossible to find in the off seasons, and when they are in season they cost a little more. Are they worth it? You bet they are! The flavors, aroma, colors, texture, and meaty centers are exceptional. These tomatoes go so well with the toasted cumin seed vinaigrette. In fact, cumin goes with tomatoes wonderfully. This salad is really one of my favorites. I only make it in the summer when heirlooms are available. Now, if you have a greenhouse, grow your own year round. The goat cheese you choose depends on your taste. I like the goat cheese that is soft in log form and sealed in plastic; it also comes that way coated in herbs, sundried tomatoes, or even dried fruit. The log is 6 in. long, and the taste is creamy, tart, and melts in your mouth. To prepare this salad, start by marinating the chicken in some of the cumin seed vinaigrette for 4 to 6 hours. I guess to start this salad make the vinaigrette first. Cut the heirloom tomatoes in half, remove the seeds, cut into bite size pieces, cut the sun gold or cherry tomatoes in half, add to the heirloom tomatoes, cook the bacon crisp drain, save the grease for vinaigrettes or cooking, crumble the bacon into the tomatoes, dice, or julienne, cut the red onion, and add it to the tomato mix. In the center of large dinner plates place the baby greens' top with the tomato mix, add the dried cherries, crumble the goat cheese over the salad after grilling the chicken slice or dice, place on top of the salad, drizzle with the cumin seed, vinaigrette, or serve on the side. And, of course, this salad can be served with everything including the chicken tossed in the vinaigrette served on large dinner plates or in a bowl served for a buffet. What, no nuts? Yes, they can be added as well as sunflower seeds or soy beans.

Toasted Cumin Seed Vinaigrette

2 T. whole cumin seed
2 t. garlic
1 c. red wine vinegar
1 c. evoo
1 c. canola, salad, or vegetable oil
1 T. dijon mustard
1/2 t. ks
1 t. fgbp

To toast the cumin seeds place a small skillet on the stove, heat the skillet, add the whole cumin seeds, and stir for about 1 minute or 2, stirring constantly so they do not burn. When the cumin seeds start to smell really awesome and take on a toasted color, turn off the heat, remove from pan, and let it cool completely before adding to the other ingredients. If you add them while they are hot the oils may splatter on you. Add all of the ingredients together and blend well. This is another vinaigrette that crushed red chilies really add zing to.

Wanda M. Raspberry Waldorf

3 c. Baby greens
3 c. Romaine lettuce
1 c. Red raspberries
1 c. Dried cherries (the recipe for making dried fruit is in the recipe for Grandma Ikie Thousand Island Chicken)
1 c. Walnut halves (toasted the recipe to toast nuts is in the recipe for Tye Pecan Chicken)
1 ea. Red apple
2 ea. 6oz. Chicken breasts or salmon
1 c. Raspberry Red Onion Vinaigrette

This is one beautiful salad. The different shades of colors of the baby greens, reds, greens, and even yellows. Sometimes along with the dark green of the romaine lettuce give a great background to add the bright red of the raspberries; the dark, deep red of the dried cherries; the golden amber of the toasted walnuts with the red and white of the apple topped with a beautifully grilled chicken breast all drizzled with the red raspberry red onion vinaigrette. Color! Color! Color! Not only is this salad to beautiful to eat, but the layers of flavors are just amazing. I suggest the chicken be marinated in apple juice and garlic for 4 to 6 hours before grilling. This salad really needs to be plated on a large, white dinner plate. The white plate really makes the colors of this salad pop. Square, white plates would really be fantastic.

I use plates of all shapes and color. My three favorite are large, white, and round, large square red with black edges and large, round, black plates. Everything looks great on all of these types of plates. Salads made with lighter-color cabbages and lettuces look better on the black plates. You do not have to pay a lot of money for plates. Discount stores are a great place to buy them. A lot of times they can be bought in sets of four place settings for about $10 or discontinued single plates for $1 to $5 each. To make this salad, first decide what two large dinner plates to use. Toss the baby greens with the romaine lettuce, place in the center of the plates, cut the apple in half, remove the core slice both halves into 5 or 6 slices, and fan half (to do this gently press on top of the sliced apple halve until the slices spread out like a fan) on each plate at the top of the plate. Scatter the raspberries, dried cherries, and toasted walnuts over the lettuce. After grilling the chicken, place one breast on each plate on the right or left side of the plate. This makes it possible to see the beautiful colors of the raspberries, dried cherries, and walnut's on top of the colors of the lettuce. Serve the vinaigrette on the side. This way everyone can enjoy the beauty of this salad before the vinaigrette covers it all up.

Raspberry Red Onion Vinaigrette

1 c. raspberry or rice wine vinegar
1 1/2 c. raspberries (fresh or frozen)
1 c. sugar
1 c. red onion
1 c. canola, salad, or vegetable oil
1 c. evoo
1 T. thyme
1 T. oregano
1 T. basil
1 T. dijon mustard
1 t. ks
1 t. fgbp

If this ingredient list looks familiar it is because it is the same ingredients list for the raspberry vinaigrette in another recipe. The only difference is red onion is added. I have not duplicated any vinaigrettes in this book for any recipe; I simply change or add one to two ingredients, and I have a new recipe. To make this vinaigrette, add all the ingredients together either in a container using a handheld blender or put it in an electric blender.

Mike J. Sweet French

2 c. Arugula
2 c. Spinach
2 c. Baby greens
12 ea. Strawberries
1 c. Blueberries
1 c. Candied pecans (the recipe for candied pecans is in the recipe for Grandma Ikie Thousand Island Chicken)
2 ea. 6 oz. Chicken breasts or salmon steaks
1 c. Sweet French Vinaigrette *(Janie's Simply Entrée)*

The combination of arugula, spinach, and baby greens makes a sweet, peppery taste. I do not care for iceberg lettuce. I think it is tasteless, ugly, and has no nutritional value at all. Arugula, spinach, and baby greens are full of flavor, vitamins, minerals, and other nutrients I cannot spell or say. The other ingredients in this salad will add plenty of flavor and nutrients. Goat cheese again? Does this woman know any other kind of cheese? Yes, I do; sheep cheese works well with this salad. I just love the soft, creamy goat cheese with its tart taste. It goes so well with sweet French vinaigrette. If you do not like soft goat cheese or sheep cheese, use whatever cheese you like. These recipes are my suggestions for what goes together; take them and create your own tastes. One thing that really improves the taste of this salad and most others is to marinate the chicken, fish, beef, pork, or seafood before grilling, baking, or roasting. There is a spicy marinade recipe in the recipe for Stan Pineapple BLT. There are a lot of vinaigrettes in this book that are great marinades; be careful of the fruit ones because the meat will burn easily from the sugars in the fruits. If you use a marinade that has vinegar or fruit juice in it, do not marinade for more than 6 hrs. The acid will cause the meat to break down, making it mushy in some cases. If you purchase a store-bought marinade make sure that water, salt, and sweetener of some sort are not the first ingredients. Now, on to the salad. First, decide if you are using chicken or salmon and then what to marinade your choice in. The chicken or salmon can be cooked two to three days ahead. I like to use large dinner plates for this salad. Toss the arugula, spinach, and baby greens together, cut the strawberries in 1/4 or slice them. Add to the lettuce mix. Next add the blue berries and candied pecans. (If you do not like pecans try cashews or walnuts, or if you do not like candied nuts use them toasted or untoasted. If you do not eat candied nuts because you are diabetic, use a sugar substitute; that works great.) The goat cheese can be sliced or crumbled then added to the salad mix. Next decide if you are slicing or dicing the chicken or salmon. Add to salad mix. Pour on the vinaigrette and toss carefully so you do not mash the berries. Place in the center of the dinner plates and enjoy. This salad can also be plated with the vinaigrette on the side or drizzled on top. More nuts and or cheese can be added to the top to garnish.

Sweet French Vinaigrette

1 c. chili sauce
1/2 c. white onion
1 t. garlic
1 1/3 c. canola oil
3/4 c. cider vinegar
1 t. paprika
1/4 c. sugar
1/8 t. worcestershire sauce
1/4 t. ks
1/2 t. fgbp

You will be amazed by how good this French vinaigrette is. You will never eat bottled French again! To make this vinaigrette, simply combine all the ingredients and blend well. This vinaigrette is thicker than most; it really sticks to what it is put on. Chili peppers can be added for extra kick.

Try using this vinaigrette for a macaroni salad or potato salad. You will be amazed!

Arthur Peanut Fruit

6 c. Baby greens
1 c. Raspberries
1 c. Black berries
1 c. Peanuts (toasted the directions to toast nuts is in the recipe for Tye Pecan Chicken)
1 c. Honeydew
1 c. Pineapple
1 c. Cantaloupe
1 c. Red or green grapes
1 c. Camembert cheese
1 c. St. Andre cheese
2 ea. 6 oz. Chicken breasts
1 c. Peanut Vinaigrette *(Janie's Simply Entrée)*

All this fruit and berries with peanuts? Next time you make a fresh fruit salad try adding some toasted peanuts. You will be very pleased with the taste. You do not like peanuts? Try cashews or almonds. The peanut vinaigrette can be made with either of those nuts instead of peanuts, but of course you have to change the name of the vinaigrette. Cashew vinaigrette or almond vinaigrette does sound good. You never know until you try! Or try a combination of two or three different nuts. Camembert and St. Andre's cheeses—where do I find them? Most food stores have them in with the specialty cheeses. They are both a soft, creamy cheese like brie. To make this salad, start with a large mixing bowl. Add the baby greens, berries, and peanuts. Peel and dice the honeydew, pineapple, and cantaloupe—the directions to peel the melons and pineapple are in the recipe for Janie S. Fire Roasted Fruit & Chicken—add to the salad mix. Next cut the grapes in 1/2 or leave whole. Dice the cheese. (These cheeses are soft and will stick to the knife. Try dipping the knife in warm water between cuts.) Add to the salad mix. This is another great salad for which to use up leftover chicken. No matter if you use fresh-cooked or leftover, dice the chicken add to all the other ingredients pour on the peanut vinaigrette. Toss well. Be careful not to smash the berries. Serve on two large dinner plates or two large salad bowls. More peanuts can be scattered on top. This salad can also be plated with the chicken sliced and placed on top then drizzled with the vinaigrette or vinaigrette on the side.

Peanut Vinaigrette

1 c. rice wine vinegar
1 c. peanut butter
1 c. toasted peanuts
1/2 c, sugar
1/2 c. canola, salad or vegetable oil
1/2 c. sesame oil
3 T. soy sauce
1 1/2 t. ginger
2 t. garlic

If this recipe looks familiar, it is because it is the recipe for the Peanut Chipotle Sesame Vinaigrette in the recipe for Matt S. Peanuts, Berries, Cheese, & Chipotle without the chipotle. As I have said before, change one ingredient, and you have created a whole new recipe to enjoy.

This vinaigrette takes a little longer to blend. If you have ever made homemade peanut butter you know what I mean. The peanuts will not completely blend. This vinaigrette will have the texture of being creamy with sand, but fear not, for the taste is great, and unlike sand the peanuts do chew well. Toast the peanuts; it deepens the taste. Peel and cut the ginger into small pieces. It will not chop well if you do not. Simply add all of the ingredients together and blend well.

Linda C. Roma Bleu Cheese

6 c. Arugula
4 ea. Roma tomatoes
1 c. Bleu cheese crumbles
1 c. Strawberries
1 c. Raspberries
1 c. Almonds (toasted the directions to do this are in
the recipe Tye Pecan Chicken)
2 ea. 6oz Chicken breasts or tuna steaks
1 c. Lemon Thyme Vinaigrette *(Simply Vinaigrettes)*

Peppery, tart, tangy, crunchy, and sweet? This salad just may be interesting. The peppery taste is from the arugula, and the tart and tangy is from the bleu cheese and lemon thyme vinaigrette. Hey, that is a whole new idea for a vinaigrette—bleu cheese lemon thyme vinaigrette; it's the crunch from the almonds and the sweet from the fruit. Try marinating the chicken or tuna in some of the lemon thyme vinaigrette for 4 to 6 hrs. before cooking. While the chicken or tuna is cooking, slice the roma tomatoes. Place half of the slices on each of two large dinner plates. Arrange around the outer edge of the plates and drizzle the roma tomato slices with some of the vinaigrette. Toss the arugula, bleu cheese, strawberries (slice or 1/4), raspberries, and almonds in the lemon thyme vinaigrette in a large mixing bowl. Place 1/2 of arugula mix on each plate. Slice the chicken or tuna. Lay across the top of the salad. Drizzle chicken or tuna with more vinaigrette. More bleu cheese crumbles can be added on top of the chicken or tuna as well as more almonds. To plate this salad without tossing, use two large dinner plates, slice the roma tomatoes, arrange around outer edge of plates, and drizzle with some of the vinaigrette. Then in the center of the plate put the arugula top with the bleu cheese crumbles, berries, and almonds. Slice the cooked chicken or tuna. Either lay it across the salad or arrange it around the plate, laying slices from center out. Then serve the vinaigrette on the side or drizzle over salad. Again, more bleu cheese and/or almonds can be sprinkled over the top.

Lemon Thyme Vinaigrette

1 c. fresh lemon juice
1 T. thyme (fresh, frozen or dried)
1 c. evoo
1 c. canola, salad, or vegetable oil
1 t. garlic
1 T. dijon mustard
1/2 c. sugar
1/4 t. ks
1/2 t. fgbp

What do you mean, I have to squeeze lemons! Well you cannot make lemon vinaigrette without them. I guess you could buy that already bottled stuff that was bottled, what, a year ago? Bottled will work, but it is just not fresh. To make this vinaigrette, add all the ingredients together, and blend to taste. If you want less sweetness and more tart add more lemon juice 1 t. at a time, and do the same if you want more sweetness; add sugar 1 t. at a time. Artificial sweetener can also be used in place of the sugar. To make this a bleu cheese lemon thyme vinaigrette, simply add 1 c. bleu cheese crumbles mix in by hand—unless you want no chunks, just creamy, then use hand blender or electric blender.

Charlotte Apple Crisp

6 c. Romaine lettuce

1 ea. Apple (your choice)

1 c. Celery hearts

1 c. Pecans (toasted or candied the directions to toast nuts is in the recipe for Tye Pecan Chicken and the directions to make candied nuts is in the recipe for Ikie Thousand Island Chicken)

12 ea. Grape or cherry tomatoes

1 c. Swiss cheese

1/2 c Bacon

2 ea. 6oz. Chicken breast or pork chops (boneless)

1 c. Fat Free Apple Rosemary Vinaigrette (recipe follows)

Apple crisp, is that not a dessert? Why no! Not in my recipe book, anyway. I named it apple crisp because it is apple and crisp. I choose romaine lettuce because it is crisp, hearty, and holds up well to other foods and vinaigrettes. There are many varieties of apples to use, red, green, yellow, sweet, and tart; follow your taste buds. I choose celery hearts because they are sweeter than the outer stalks. The pecans can be toasted or candied the choice is yours. If you do not like cherry or grape tomatoes, use the ones you do like. If you use large tomatoes, cut in half and remove the seeds before dicing. If you do use grape or cherry, cut in half or leave whole. The swiss cheese I chose because it is a fairly firm cheese, and the flavor goes very well with apple. Other cheeses that go well with apple are, in my opinion, gouda, bleu cheese, havarti, and cheddar. The cheese I either dice or shred. When it comes to bacon I like apple wood, smoked, thick, sliced, and cooked crisp. Save the bacon grease for vinaigrettes or other cooking. This salad is also a great way to use leftover chicken or pork. Okay, let's make this salad. I like to toss this salad with the vinaigrette and serve it in large salad bowls. Cut the romaine lettuce into bite-size pieces and wash. Spin or pat dry place in a large mixing bowl, dice the apple, toss with a little of the vinaigrette or lemon water to help slow down the browning process, add to the romaine, cut the celery either into slices or dice it, add the pecans, add the grape or cherry tomatoes to the party in the mixing bowl, shred or dice the cheese, add to other stuff, crumble the bacon into the mix, dice or shred the chicken or pork, and add it to the bowl. Now pour on the vinaigrette, toss well, and place in the salad bowls.

Fat Free Apple Rosemary Vinaigrette

1 ea. apple (your choice of variety)
2 c. apple juice (sweetened or unsweetened)
1 c. apple cider vinegar
1 T. sugar or sugar substitute
1 t/ ks
1 t. fgbp

I do not peel the apple for this vinaigrette. The flecks of skin add color and are very small. Cut up the apple and remove the core. Place everything together in a container when using handheld blender or an electric blender. Blend well. Taste for sweetness, and add salt and pepper. Adjust accordingly; just remember if you add more sugar do 1/2 t. at a time. If you desire more apple, taste it and add another apple. Applesauce can be used as well as apple jelly. This is another vinaigrette that is fantastic with some heat such as jalapenos or crushed red chilies. This is also great used for a marinade for grilling chicken, pork, or fish.

Glenda Green Goddess Berry

6 c. Baby greens
1 c. Strawberries
1 c. Blueberries
1 c. Red raspberries
1 ea. Banana
1 c. Walnut (halves toasted the directions for toasting
   nuts is in the recipe for Tye Pecan Chicken)
12 ea. Grape or cherry tomatoes
1 c. Janie's Green Goddess Dressing (recipe follows)

My gosh! This green goddess is a dressing that's an oldie yet a goodie. What? No chicken or beef for this salad? No! I made it vegetarian, but you sure can add chicken, beef, pork, seafood, or fish. This is a very simple salad to make. In a mixing bowl, add the baby greens, strawberries (either slice or 1/4 them), add blueberries and red raspberries, slice the banana, add the walnuts, cut the tomatoes in half or leave whole, add the green goddess dressing, toss well, and make sure you do not smash the berries or banana. Place on large dinner plates or salad bowls. Maybe garnish with more berries and nuts. Some nice fruit bread with honey butter would be great with this salad or even start with a bowl of homemade tomato soup.

Janie's Green Goddess Dressing

I could not find a recipe I liked, so I played with the ingredients until I found the right combination for me. Most of them were complicated; this is not a complicated dressing.

1 t. garlic
5 ea. Or 1 T. anchovies (whole or paste)
1 bnch. parsley (curly or Italian)
2 T. lemon juice
2 T. tarragon vinegar
2 c. mayonnaise (fresh made or processed the recipe to make mayonnaise is in the recipe for Alicia Curried Chicken)
1 c. sour cream
1 t. fgbp

You notice there is no salt added; there is plenty in the anchovies, but if you want more add more. The parsley leaves need to be removed from the stems. The parsley is to make the color green. Most of recipes I looked at before coming up with my own said to chop the parsley, put in cheese cloth, and squeeze out the green color into the dressing mixture. I just added it. Put everything together in a container for a hand blender to be used or in an electric blender and blend well. This will keep for two weeks in the fridge. If you make your own mayonnaise. If you use commercial made it will last a month. Dressings like this are best if made in small batches.

Rebecca Island Breeze

6 c. Baby greens

2 c. Pineapple (the directions for peeling pineapple is in the recipe for Janie S. Fire Roasted Fruit & Chicken)

1 ea. Banana

1 c. Candied pecans (the recipe for making candied nuts is in the recipe for Grandma Ikie Thousand Island Chicken)

1 c. Green onions

2 c. Tomatoes (large salad, grape, cherry or roma)

1 c. Smoked ham

2 ea. 6oz. Chicken breasts

1 c. Sweet herb marinade (recipe follows)

1 c. Poppy Seed Green Onion Vinaigrette (recipe follows)

Bananas again? Yes, bananas are not just for banana splits any more. They go so well with all sorts of foods. Pineapple, green onions, and tomatoes, oh yeah! They make a great salsa also. I will give you a recipe for it following this recipe. The directions I give will be for plating this salad with the vinaigrette on the side; of course, this salad can also be tossed. Use two large dinner plates, place the baby greens in the center of the plate, dice the pineapple, scatter over the greens, slice the banana, scatter over the greens on both plates, slice the green onions from tip to end using all the onion, and if you use large salad or roma tomatoes cut them in half and remove seeds. Dice into bite size pieces, scatter over the salad, julienne cut or dice the ham, and add it to the salad. The sweet herb marinade is for marinating the chicken for 4 to 6 hrs. before grilling. After cooking the chicken either slice or dice the chicken place on top of the salad. Serve the vinaigrette on the side or drizzle over the salad. More pecans can be tossed on top. Shrimp is also great on this salad, as is crab meat or lobster.

Sweet Herb Marinade

1/2 c. sugar
1 t. dried basil
1 t. dried oregano
1 t. dried thyme
1/2 t. ks
1 t. fgbp
Canola, salad, or vegetable oil

Mix all the dry ingredients together, place in a sealable plastic bag or container with tight lid. A larger quantity can be mixed for later use. This dry mix can be kept in a dry place until used. To use this dry mix take all the dry ingredients listed above mix with 1 c. of oil. Mix well in a container with a lid that the chicken breasts will fit in. Toss the chicken well in the marinade to coat. Place lid on the container and put in the fridge for at least 4 to 6 hrs. The chicken can set in this marinade for up to five days to marinade before cooking. There is no vinegar or acid to break down the chicken. Toss out the marinade after use.

Poppy Seed Green Onion Vinaigrette

1 c. sugar
1 1/2 t. ks
1/2 t. fgbp
1 c. cider vinegar
2 c. canola, salad or vegetable oil
1/2 c. green onion
2 T. poppy seeds

Cut the green onions in pieces no more than 1/4 in. long from tip to end. Use entire onion. If you do not cut them small they will not chop up but only wrap in strings around blade. I know; I learned the hard way. Add all of the ingredients together, blend well with either a handheld blender or an electric blender. If the green onion taste is not strong enough for you, add more and do the same with the sugar, salt, and pepper.

Pineapple Green Onion & Tomato Salsa

Here it is the salsa recipe I promised you. I give no amounts for this; it depends on the flavor you want. If you want more pineapple, use more pineapple—the same for more green onions and more tomatoes. You get the idea. The heat depends on how much fresh jalapeno you add. You can use canned jalapenos if you want to. I prefer fresh. Also, canned pineapple can be used as well as canned tomatoes. I do suggest to begin with you use equal amounts of pineapple, green onion, tomato, and banana with 1 jalapeno for each cup of the other ingredients combined. Salt and pepper is up to your taste. This salsa will keep for no more than a few days in the fridge before the banana goes bad. The rest of the ingredients will last at least a week. The salsa can be made without the banana, but add it when needed.

pineapple
green onion
tomato
banana
jalapeno
ks.
fgbp.
cilantro (optional)
garlic (optional)

I hope you enjoy this simple salsa recipe. Also, chipotles can be used as well as habaneros. All the ingredients can be diced the size you want or blended together. If you add cilantro remove the stems from the leaves. Use as little or as much as you like. Do the same with the garlic; add if you like.

Nate S. Flat Bread Ham & Egg

2 ea. Pita bread or flat bread
1 c. Ham salad *(Janie's Simply Entrée)*
1 c. Egg salad *(Janie's Simply Entrée)*
6 c. Fresh spinach
12 ea. Grape tomatoes
1 c. Green Onion Vinaigrette (recipe follows)

Is this a salad or a sandwich? I consider it a salad because of the way it is put together. Pita bread and flatbread are actually the same thing. This is a nice lunch or early dinner by the pool. Even kids like this one. The flatbread, as I will refer to it, can be heated on a grill, on the stove, or on a flat-top griddle. This salad looks great on a beautiful, large dinner plate of black or red. Toss the spinach and tomatoes in the green onion vinaigrette; the tomatoes can be cut in half or left whole. Place this in the center of the plates, toast the flat bread, and cut each in four pieces. Now you have 8 pieces of flatbread. Put ham salad on 4 pieces and egg salad on the other 4 pieces. Lay 2 pieces of each on both salad plates on top of the spinach and tomatoes. Thin, sliced green onion can be used to garnish the ham-and-egg salads.

Green Onion Vinaigrette

2 T. garlic
12 ea. green onions
1 T. basil (dried or fresh)
1 1/2 t. thyme (dried or fresh)
2 t. dijon mustard
1 c. rice wine vinegar
1 c. canola, salad or vegetable oil
1 c. evoo
1/2 t. ks
1/2 t. fgbp
1 T. sugar

Cut the green onions from tip to end in pieces about 1/4 in. long. This will prevent the green onions from stringing and wrapping around the blades. Combine everything together; blend well.

Ham Salad

I do not give quantities because it depends on how much you want; extra always comes in handy. Besides, who can make enough ham salad for only two people? Also, on about the third day after you make it the flavor is awesome.

ham (dice, chop, or grind)
mayonnaise (fresh made or processed the recipe to make mayonnaise is in the recipe for Alicia Curried Chicken)
sweet pickle relish or sweet pickles
white onion
fgbp.

If you have a food processor or one of those metal food grinders that attach to the table or counter you have the right equipment. I like to use a food processor. I place the ham, mayonnaise, onion, and relish in the food processor. Add the pepper, put on lid, turn on, and let blend. The mayonnaise helps the ham to process. If you like it chunky, chop with a knife or only chop in the food processor on pulse. Add the rest of the ingredients and mix well. Mustard or curry powder can be added for a different taste. Do not keep for more than 6 to 7 days before tossing out.

Egg Salad

hard cooked eggs
onion
mayonnaise (homemade or processed the recipe to make mayonnaise is in the recipe for Alicia Curried Chicken)
celery
dijon mustard
tabasco sauce
worcestershire sauce
ks.
fgbp.

I have done this recipe the same way I did the ham salad with no quantities; the rule I usually use is 2 eggs per person, and the amount of celery and onion depends on your taste. I like lots of fine, diced celery and onion. To hard cook the eggs, put fresh eggs in a sauce pan and cover with cold water. Put it on the stove and let it come to a full boil. Cover the pan turn off the heat. Let it set for 12 min. When done cooking drain place in ice water to stop cooking. Peel the eggs and either chop with a knife or an egg slicer into a mixing bowl. As I said I like lots of celery and onion diced very small. Add to the eggs and add the dijon mustard, tabasco, worcestershire, mayonnaise, salt and pepper. Mix well. Do not keep any unused egg salad for more than five days. The eggs and onion will go bad before the mayonnaise if you used commercially processed mayonnaise. Fresh made mayonnaise needs to be really taken care of for refrigeration. I hope you enjoy my egg salad, and as with the ham salad, curry powder can be added for a great change in taste. Cheese is also great mixed into egg salad.

Chuck O. Spicy Sweet Italian

6 c. Romaine lettuce
2 ea. Roma tomatoes
1 c. Pepperoni
1 c. Salami
1 c. Chicken
1 c. Mozzarella cheese
10 ea. Black olives
1/2 c. Red onion
1 c. Spicy Sweet Italian Vinaigrette

There is something about spicy and sweet. They were made to go together. The romaine lettuce can be sliced or cut into bite-size pieces. The roma tomatoes can be either sliced or diced. I prefer to dice them, first. I cut them in1/2, remove the seeds, then dice. Pepperoni can be bought in different sizes, sliced, and in sticks uncut. If you bought uncut either slice or dice them. The mini pepperoni are great for this salad. There are a lot of varieties of mozzarella cheeses: fresh, block, shredded, sliced, or diced. The chicken can be diced or shredded, grilled, baked, roasted, or boiled. This is a great way to use leftover chicken. Cut the black olives in 1/2 or slice them. Don't like black olives? Use green or both. There are a lot of different olives available. Some stores have olive bars where you buy them by the pint or quart. The red onion can be sliced or diced. My favorite way to serve this salad is tossed. To do this use either large salad bowls or large dinner plates. Place all the ingredients together in a large mixing bowl. Add the vinaigrette. Toss well and place it in the salad bowls or on the plates. Add some crusty, warm bread with herb-whipped butter along with a glass of red wine, and dinner is served. To serve plated use either large salad bowls or large dinner plates. Place the romaine in the center and add all the other ingredients. Drizzle with the vinaigrette or serve on the side.

Spicy Sweet Italian Vinaigrette

1 c. red wine vinegar
2 c. evoo
1 T. Italian seasoning
1 t. garlic powder
1 t. onion powder
2 t. crushed red chilies
1/2 t. ks
1 t. fgbp

Here it is again—spicy and sweet, cannot be beat. I use garlic and onion powder in this recipe because it dissolves very well. Fresh can be used in also the same amount. Put everything together and blend well. This vinaigrette is also great as a vegetable dip or poured on steamed, roasted, or grilled vegetables.

Jim Christmas

6 c. Baby greens
1 c. Swiss cheese
2 ea. Oranges
1 c. Almonds (toasted the directions for this is in the recipe for Tye Pecan Chicken)
2 ea. 6oz. Pork loin
1 c. Sage marinade (recipe follows)
1 c. Black Berry Cranberry Sage Vinaigrette (recipe follows)

This is the perfect salad for a holiday party. Oranges, cranberries, and blackberries go great together. Swiss cheese? Why swiss cheese? Because it goes so well with cranberries! If you do not like swiss cheese try using mozzarella or provolone. Marinate the pork loin in the sage marinade for at least 4 to 6 hours overnight—or several days would be even better. This salad can be either served, tossed, or plated with the vinaigrette on the side. To make this salad tossed, place the baby greens in a large mixing bowl. The swiss can be either diced or shredded. Peel the oranges and either dice or cut out the sections. Add to the salad mix. Toss in the almonds. The pork loin can either be sliced and placed on top or diced and added to the toss mix. Pour on the vinaigrette. Toss well, and serve on either large dinner plates or in large salad bowls. To serve plated use large dinner plates and put the baby greens on the plates. Dice or shred the cheese and scatter it over the greens. Peel, dice, or cut orange into sections and place on greens. Add almonds and slice or dice the pork loin then place it on top of the salad. Drizzle with the vinaigrette or serve on the side.

Blackberry Cranberry Sage Vinaigrette

1 c. black berries
1 c. fresh cranberries or 1 c. cranberry sauce
2 t. sage (fresh or ground)
1 c. rice wine vinegar
2 c. canola, salad or vegetable oil
1/2 t ks
1/2 t. fgbp
1/4 c. sugar

What is not to love about cranberries and blackberries? Each on their own is awesome, but together—what a taste! Put everything together and blend well. If you freeze the cranberries they blend much better. If you use canned, I suggest the whole berries variety. This vinaigrette is also great for putting on grilled chicken or using as a dip for the chicken.

Sage Marinade

1 c. canola, salad or vegetable oil
1 T. fresh or ground sage
1 t. garlic (fresh or dried)
1 t. fgbp
1/2 t. ks

Mix everything together. Toss with the pork loin and let marinade for 4 to 6 hrs. or overnight. There is no vinegar or acid in this marinade, so the pork can sit in the fridge for up to five days before grilling. Discard marinade after use.

Sandy H. Bleu & Berries

3 c. Baby greens
3 c. Spinach
1 c. Blue berries
1 c. Raspberries
1 c. Bleu cheese
1 c. Candied walnuts (the directions for making candied nuts is in the recipe for Grandma Ikie Thousand Island Chicken)
2 ea. 6oz Beef steaks or chicken breasts
1 c. Strawberry Walnut Vinaigrette

Here it is again—bleu cheese and candied walnuts. They are really made for each other. I wonder if it would work out to put some bleu cheese on the candied walnuts half of the way through cooking! I may have to try it. Or bake the candied walnuts until done then sprinkle some of the bleu cheese on top and return it to the oven for maybe 2 min. but no more. My first choice of meat for this salad is beef, but chicken goes really well on it. I like to plate this salad with the vinaigrette on the side—only because it is such a beautiful salad. Select large dinner plates; white or black would work great. Place the baby greens and spinach in the center of the plates and add the berries, bleu cheese, and candied walnuts. Then slice the beef steaks. Lay that across the salad, and more bleu cheese can be scattered over the warm steak.

Strawberry Walnut Vinaigrette

2 c. strawberries (fresh or frozen)
1 c. walnuts (toasted the directions for this are in the recipe for Tye Pecan Chicken)
1 c. rice wine vinegar
1 c. evoo
1 c. canola, salad or vegetable oil
1/2 c. sugar
1/2 t. ks
1 t. fgbp

Why toast the walnuts to blend in a vinaigrette? To bring out the oils, making the flavor more intense. The strawberries can be fresh or frozen IQF (individually quick frozen). The ones that are sold frozen cooked will not work. Neither will strawberry jam. Put all the ingredients together, blend well, and enjoy. This vinaigrette is great for use on grilled chicken or pork as a glaze or dip. Jalapenos, habaneros, or other chilies can be added for extra zip.

John Curried Egg Salad Sandwich with Sweet Tarragon Red Wine Slaw

Curried Egg Salad

3 ea. hard cooked eggs
1/4 c. red onion
1/2 t. tabasco sauce
1/2 t. worcestershire sauce
1/2 t. ks
1 t. fgbp
1 to 2 T. curry powder
1/2 to 1 c. mayonnaise (fresh made or processed the recipe to make this is in the recipe for Alicia Curried Chicken)

The directions for cooking the eggs hard boiled are in the recipe for Nate Flat Bread Ham & Egg Salad. This egg salad recipe is different from the recipe for egg salad in Nate Flat Bread Ham & Egg Salad. I have tried putting the hard cooked eggs in a food processor to make egg salad. Well, it was not a good thing; the texture was like sand—really fine, almost like baby food. So I suggest using an egg slicer or a fork to mash the eggs into a mixing bowl. Fine dice the red onion, add to the eggs, add the tabasco sauce and worcestershire sauce, salt, pepper, curry powder, and 1/2 c. of mayonnaise. Mix well. Taste and add more curry or other ingredients to suit your taste. Curried egg salad is also great served in a tomato or by itself on top of baby greens, spinach, or cabbage with some of the sweet tarragon red wine vinaigrette drizzled over the top. Tomatoes, cucumber, and carrots can be added.

Sweet Tarragon Red Wine Slaw

2 c. shredded cabbage (green head, nappa or both)
1/2 c shredded carrots
1/2 c. cucumbers
1/4 c. red onion
1/4 t. ks
1/2 t. fgbp
1/2 c. sweet tarragon red wine vinaigrette (recipe follows)

Shred the cabbage very fine. Peel, and shred the carrots. Rinse under cold water until there is no more orange color in the water. If you do not, your slaw will be orange. The cucumber can be peeled or left unpeeled. Either way, cut in half the long way and remove the seeds and either fine slice or dice. Add to cabbage, slice the red onion very thinly, add to the cabbage add the salt and pepper mix in the vinaigrette and toss well. This slaw is better made 1 to 2 days ahead of time. The quantities for this recipe can be increased to make a buffet salad or to use it as a side dish with barbeque chicken or ribs.

Sweet Tarragon Red Wine Vinaigrette

1/2 c. red wine vinegar
1/2 c. sugar or sugar substitute
1 c. canola, salad or vegetable oil
1 t. dijon mustard
1/2 t. garlic
1/4 t. ks
1/2 t. fgbp

Combine everything together and blend well. This vinaigrette is better after it sets for one week in the fridge. This vinaigrette is also great for use on sub sandwiches.

Curried Egg Salad Sandwich

2 ea. Ciabatta bread rolls
2 c. Curried egg salad (recipe above)
4 ea. Slices of tomato
2 c. Sweet tarragon red wine slaw (recipe above)
2 ea. Kosher dill pickles
4 ea. Sandwich picks

Slice the rolls in half. Toast in a skillet on the stove or grill. Lay the rolls on a flat surface. On the bottom piece of bread, place 1/2 the egg salad, 2 slices of tomato, and 1/2 of the sweet tarragon red wine slaw. Place the top on the roll. Place 2 sandwich picks in each sandwich. Cut the sandwiches in 1/2. Place on two large dinner plates and garnish with kosher dill pickles. Serve with a side of the Keith Red Skin Potato Salad.

Dwanett Baked or Grilled Chicken Sandwich with Apple Orange Cabbage Slaw

Apple Orange Cabbage Slaw

1 c. green cabbage

1 c. nappa cabbage

1/4 c. peanuts (the recipe for toasting nuts is in the recipe for Tye Pecan Chicken)

1/2 c. diced tomatoes

1/2 c. mandarin oranges

1/2 c. raisins

1/2 t. ks

1/2 t. fgbp

1 c. apple vinaigrette (recipe follows)

Shred the cabbage very thin, add the peanuts, cut the tomato in half, remove seeds, dice fine, drain the mandarin oranges, save the juice for baking, add to the cabbage mix, and add the raisins, salt, and pepper. Pour on the vinaigrette and mix well. This slaw is also better when made 2 to 3 days ahead of time. This slaw also can be made in a larger serving for a buffet salad or a side dish with just about anything. Add chicken or pork tossed in or served on top to make a complete meal.

Apple Vinaigrette

1/2 c apple juice or apple cider
1 c. apple cider vinegar or use all apple juice
2 ea. red or green apples 1 c. evoo
1 c. canola, salad or vegetable oil
1 to 2 T. sugar
1/2 t. ks
1 t. fgbp

You can make this vinaigrette with all apple juice or part apple juice and apple cider. Do not peel the apples; just cut it in pieces and combine everything together. Blend well. There will be small flecks of apple peel in the vinaigrette; it really looks great. Start with 1 T. sugar then taste and add more if needed. To make this vinaigrette fat free replace the oil with apple juice. I find unsweetened works great for my taste; I like the crisp, tart taste. This vinaigrette will be very thin, so add 1/8 t. of xanthan gum. That should do the trick. Use more if needed.

Baked or Grilled Chicken Sandwich

2 ea. 6oz. Chicken breasts
4 ea. Slices of rye bread
2 c. Apple orange cabbage slaw (recipe above)
Sweet pickles
1 c. Apple Vinaigrette (recipe above)
4 ea. Sandwich picks

Marinade the chicken in the apple vinaigrette for 4 to 6 hrs. before cooking. Any longer will cause the vinegar and apple juice to break down the proteins in the chicken too much, and the chicken could be mushy. The bread can be toasted. Lay the chicken breasts on two slices of rye bread. Top with the apple orange cabbage slaw and place on the top slices of bread. Put 2 sandwich picks in each sandwich. Cut in half. Serve with sweet pickles. Serve with a side of macaroni salad. Try the recipe for Nate H. Macaroni Salad.

Rick S. Curried Seafood Sandwich

I have broken up the recipe. First I give the directions for making the curried seafood then for making the sandwich. If you do not like curry replace the curry with cocktail sauce. I will give a recipe for making a fast, easy one. There are also a lot of vinaigrettes in this book that would be great used for this seafood salad such as the thousand island, sweet French, or cayenne pepper vinaigrettes, just leave out the mayonnaise and curry. Add the vinaigrette instead.

Curried Seafood

1 c. shrimp
1 c. crab meat (real or imitation)
1/2 c. celery
1/2 c. green onions
2 to 4 T. curry powder
4 T. mayonnaise (homemade or processed the recipe to make mayonnaise is in the recipe for Alicia Curried Chicken)
1 t. tabasco sauce
1 t. worcestershire sauce
1/2 t. ks.
1 t. fgbp

If you really like curry you will like this sandwich. The shrimp you use depends on how hard you want to work. Already cooked shrimp is available in the frozen section of any food store. They are available in a variety of sizes; the tiny baby shrimp are great for this salad because you do not have to cut them up. If you use a size, say, 21 to 25 you have to cut them up into bite-size pieces (I explain the sizing of shrimp in the recipe Martin Very Berry Coconut Shrimp). To cook your own shrimp bring plenty of water to a boil and add salt and lemon (either fresh cut in half or lemon juice, not a lot of juice—maybe 2 T). I also like to use pickling spice and raw onion. If you do not have pickling spice, pepper and lemon juice will work. When water is boiling add shrimp peeled or with skin on and let it return to boil. Turn off the heat and wait for 8 minutes. Check with a knife, cutting down backside to see if shrimp is done. If it is, remove from hot water and put in ice water to stop cooking and cool down. Cut shrimp into desired size. Put in a towel to wring out and remove excess water. If you do not, your salad will be runny. Place in a mixing bowl. If you are using real crab meat from a can check with hands to make sure there are no shells in it. After checking for shells wrap in a towel and squeeze to remove excess water. Also, break it up into small pieces. If you use imitation crab (it is made from fish) squeeze out excess water, also. I have never cooked a fresh crab, but it does not look hard. If you do, after cooking place it in ice water to chill down so you can remove the meat. No matter what crab you use add to the shrimp, fine dice the celery, slice the green onions thin, and add the curry, the mayonnaise, tabasco, worcestershire sauce, and salt and pepper. Mix well. Taste. Add more curry or any of the other ingredients to adjust the taste you are looking for. Serve well chilled. Discard any unused after 4 to 5 days. Seafood goes bad very fast. For a delicious salad made from this curried seafood add some fresh spinach, cabbage, or baby greens with some tomatoes. Toss together or serve the curried seafood on top of your choice of spinach, cabbage, baby greens, or all of them mixed together. Remember anything you can put on bread to make a great sandwich can be put with lettuces, spinach, cabbages or arugula to make a great salad.

Curried Seafood Sandwich

4 ea. Slices of bread (any variety white, wheat, rye, whole grain, sour dough, sub rolls, or croissants)
4 ea. Tomato slices
2 ea. Leaves of lettuce (romaine, Iceberg, red leaf, oak leaf, green leaf, or a handful of baby greens, spinach, or arugula)
2 c. Curried seafood salad (recipe above)
4 ea. Sandwich picks

I really like my sandwiches on bread that has been toasted either in a toaster, toaster oven, or even in a skillet on the stove. I really like it toasted on both sides. Sub rolls or croissants can be put in the toaster oven, under the broiler in your oven, or in a skillet on the stove. Just make sure you butter them first; it makes them more crunchy. If you do not like butter use evoo, or even mayonnaise works great if you like mayonnaise. I also toast both sides of the bread but only butter or evoo the side that will be out. This prevents the bread from getting soggy as fast if the food going on it is mixed with mayonnaise or a dressing or vinaigrette of some sort. The gas, charcoal, or wood grills work great, also. After you have toasted your bread of choice, lay it on a flat surface. I like to lay the lettuce down first then the tomato slices then a generous scoop of the curry seafood mix. It does not matter if you use an actual ice cream scoop or a spoon; fill it with the curry seafood squeeze against the inside of the bowl to remove the excess liquid. This helps the bread from getting soggy. But then again my mom always said a sandwich or burger is not good if it does not make a mess, and I agree. If you like your sandwich with slaw on it, try adding the Sweet Tarragon Red Wine Slaw or the Apple Orange Cabbage Slaw on the sandwich instead of the lettuce and tomato or as a side. Add the top slice of bread. After you have made this great sandwich add 2 sandwich picks to each. Cut in half and place on 2 large dinner plates with sweet pickles or a spicy pickle mix on the side. Pickled okra is also great with this sandwich.

Simple Cocktail Sauce

1 c. chili sauce
1 T. horseradish
1/2 t. ks
1/2 t. fgbp
1 T. lemon juice
4 drops tabasco sauce
3 drops worcestershire sauce

Chili sauce—where do I find chili sauce? It is in the isle with the tabasco, worcestershire, steak sauces, etc., next to the jars of cocktail sauce. Well, why can I not buy a jar of already made cocktail sauce? You can; it is just better to make yourself. If you want more horseradish add more, same with the tabasco and worcestershire sauces. Put everything in a bowl, mix well, and enjoy. Oh, by the way, you can use ketchup instead of chili sauce or use it along with it.

Robert Mandarin Orange Chicken Salad Sandwich

Mandarin Orange Chicken Salad

2 c. chicken meat (white or dark)
1 c. mandarin oranges
1/4 c. almonds or pecans (toasted the directions for toasting nuts is in the recipe for Tye Pecan Chicken)
1/4 c. mayonnaise (homemade or processed the recipe for making mayonnaise is in the recipe for Alicia Curried Chicken)
1/2 t. ks
1 t. fgbp

This is a great way to use leftover chicken no matter how it is cooked. If it is leftover herb roasted, that adds a lot of flavor to the salad. If you are grilling chicken for dinner tonight, and you know you will need chicken for this salad two days from now, grill extra. To make this salad dice or shred the chicken, place in a mixing bowl, open the can or jar of mandarin oranges, drain well, add to chicken, and save the liquid to make a cake, cupcakes, and even a sauce. If you can find fresh mandarin oranges you are in luck. Peel, and cut in sections. Add to chicken. Add the nuts, mayonnaise, salt, and pepper and mix well enjoy. Do not keep any leftover for more than 5 days. This mandarin orange chicken is also great on a bed of lettuce with more mandarin oranges and nuts sprinkled around the plate with maybe some tomato added—or stuffed in a tomato on top of a bed of baby greens or spinach with mandarin orange, green onion vinaigrette, or poppy seed dressing. You could also mix mandarin orange vinaigrette with poppy seed dressing or just add some mandarin oranges to the poppy seed dressing. Yes this sandwich would make a great entrée salad! I have not suggested that because there is an entrée salad in this book similar to this recipe: the Dougie Mandarin Orange.

Mandarin Orange Chicken Salad Sandwich

4 ea. Slices of bread (your choice)
2 c. Mandarin orange chicken salad (recipe above)
2 ea. Lettuce leaves
4 ea. Tomato slices
4 ea. Sandwich picks

Here again I like my bread toasted on both sides. I explained all this in the other recipe, so I will not bore you with it again. After toasting the bread lay it on a flat surface. Place the lettuce on two slices as well as the tomato slices. Top with the mandarin orange chicken salad. Place the other two slices of bread on top. Put 2 sandwich picks in each sandwich. Slice in half place on two large dinner plates with pickles or pickled vegetables of your choice. What to serve on the side? Maybe some cottage cheese with tomato slices or pasta salad.

Cora Cauliflower Cherry Pepper Relish Vegetarian Sandwich

This is one of those great vegetarian sandwiches for when you vegetarian side starts to scream. Mine starts to scream, but I can usually shut her up with a steak. Actually, I do enjoy a nice vegetarian sandwich as long as it has lots of flavor and stuff on it. I think this one does.

Vegetarian Sandwich

2 ea. Roasted red bell peppers (already roasted in a jar or fresh roasted the directions for roasting red bell peppers is in the recipe for Linda M. Chicken Pasta Salad Tossed in Sweet Tomato Vinaigrette)
4 ea. Tomato slices
2 ea. Red onion slices
12 ea. Cucumber slices
2 ea. Smoked gouda cheese slices
2 ea. Swiss cheese slices
1 c. Cauliflower cherry pepper relish (recipe follows)
2 ea. Lettuce leaves
2 ea. Crusty sub rolls
Pinch ks
Pinch fgbp
4 ea. Sandwich picks

Here, again, toast the buttered- or evoo-coated sub rolls on a hot surface or in a broiler. Lay on a flat surface. Place the lettuce leaves on the rolls and add 2 tomato slices to each. Top that with the roasted red bell peppers. If the red onion slices are large cut in 1/2. Lay both halves on each roll, and top that with 6 cucumber slices on each roll. Cut the smoked gouda cheese slices in ½, and lay two halves on each roll. On each roll, do the same with the swiss cheese. The reason I cut them in 1/2 is because they will hang off the roll. This way there are both cheeses in each bite. Top with the cauliflower cherry pepper relish. Place the tops on. Put 2 sandwich picks in each sandwich then cut in half. Place on 2 large dinner plates. Maybe serve with a mustard potato salad and a good, crisp dill pickle. Other options to add to this sandwich are grilled or roasted zucchini, eggplant, or yellow squash. Also, the tomatoes and onions can be grilled or roasted. I do not picture this sandwich as a salad; if you do that is great.

Cauliflower Cherry Pepper Relish

1 c. cauliflower
1 c. cherry peppers
1/2 c. black olives
1/2 c. red onion
1 t. garlic
1/2 t. ks
1 t. fgbp
1/4 c. balsamic vinegar
1/4 c. evoo

Cut the cauliflower into small pieces. Put in a food processor or blender. If you do not have one of these this can be chopped by hand. Cut the cherry peppers in half. Remove the membranes and seeds. Add that to the cauliflower. Add the olives. If you do not like black olives use green or whatever type of olive you like. What? You do not like olives? Okay, add celery—or nothing at all. Cut the red onion into small pieces. Add to the party and add the garlic, salt, pepper, balsamic vinegar, and evoo. You control the chop on this relish. Quick chop with chunks is nice, and more chop with much smaller chunks is fine, also. Cherry peppers are not known to be hot. If you want more heat add some jalapenos. Herbs can also be added to this relish such as dried rosemary. Fresh rosemary does not chop well; it ends up like sand. Preheat oven to 350 degrees. Place in the oven on a cookie sheet. It should not take more than 5 min. Let cool and remove from sticks. Add 1 T. to relish before blending. All herbs dry the same way in the oven. Basil, oregano, or thyme are also great. This relish is also great tossed with pasta & chicken.

Haley Sweet & Spicy Beef Wrap

1 # Beef
1 c. Onion (red or white)
1 c. Bell peppers (any color)
1 T. Garlic
2 t. Canola, salad or vegetable oil
1 t. Ks
1 t. Fgbp
1 can El Pato sauce
1/4 c. Brown sugar
2 ea. Large flour tortilla (any flavor)
1 c. Jalapeno cheese
1 c. Shredded cheddar cheese
1 c. Shredded lettuce (optional)

What is El Pato sauce, and where do I find it? It is a spicy tomato sauce sold where the Mexican food is at any grocery store. There are three varieties. I do not know the differences in them other than the can colors: yellow, green, and red. They all taste the same to me—delicious! It is very versatile and can be used for anything you use tomato sauce for. The can is the size of a small can of tomato sauce. The beef you select depends on your taste. The beef for this wrap is cut into bite-size pieces. Some suggestions I have for your meat choices are stew meat, chuck roast, and even beef scraps. The onion can be diced or julienne cut—the same goes for the bell peppers. My choice for both of these is julienne cut. The garlic is chopped small. In a large skillet, heat the oil but not to smoking. Add the meat, onions, bell peppers, and garlic sauté to brown. Add the salt-and-pepper mix well. Add the El Pato sauce and turn heat down to simmer. If you do not use all of the El Pato sauce, make a vinaigrette out of it—I give a recipe below for this. Add brown sugar. Cover. Let simmer until the meat is tender. Canned beef can also be used. Sauté the peppers and onions in the oil add the canned beef, salt, pepper, brown sugar, and El Pato sauce. Let simmer until all the liquid is gone. Warm the flour tortillas on a griddle or skillet; they wrap better if softened. Thirty seconds in the microwave will work also if you have one. Lay the warmed-up tortilla on a flat surface. Add a healthy serving of the beef mix. Place about 2 inches from the bottom. Add the cheeses and lettuce. Fold the bottom up over the beef and cheese. Fold the sides in. There should be about 2 to 3 inches on each side to fold in to the center. Then start at the bottom roll upward to form a burrito. A very small amount of oil can be put in a skillet or on a griddle to put a toasted crunch on the tortilla; make sure you place it with the flap down so it will stay rolled. Carefully roast on all sides. Beans can also be added to this wrap—whole pintos or refried as well as potatoes. Leftover bakers are great to dice up and add to the meat mix. Cut in 1/2 and place on large dinner plates. I cannot think of any side to serve with this wrap; it is a complete meal in and of itself and is very filling. To make this wrap into a salad simply place cut-up lettuce or baby greens in the center of large dinner plates. Top with the meat mix and cheeses.

Beans and potatoes can also be added. No vinaigrette is needed because of the sauce in the meat. A spicy vinaigrette can be made with the El Pato Sauce.

El Pato Vinaigrette

1 can El Pato sauce
1 c. cider vinegar
2 c. canola, salad or vegetable oil or
1 c. evoo and
1 c. canola, salad or vegetable oil
2 T. garlic
1 t. cayenne pepper
1 t. cumin
1 t. ks
1 t. fgbp

Combine everything together in a container using a handheld blender or electric blender. Blend well. You will find so many uses for this vinaigrette. Try basting chicken or ribs with this while grilling or as a vinaigrette for a pasta salad. Sugar or brown sugar and jalapeno, habanero, or coriander seed can be added to this vinaigrette, also.

Devon Italian Hoagie with Sauerkraut Relish

An Italian Hoagie with sauerkraut relish? Really! Yes! Try it; you may like it.

Italian Hoagie

2 ea. Hoagie rolls
2 c. Iceberg lettuce
4 ea. Tomato slices
6 ea. Slices salami
2 ea. Slices provolone cheese
6 ea. Slices smoked ham
2 ea. Slices mozzarella cheese
6 ea. Slices cappacola ham
1/2 c. Very thin sliced red onion
6 ea. Pepperoncini's
2 c. Sauerkraut relish (recipe follows)
4 ea. Sandwich picks

This sandwich can be made with a toasted hoagie roll served cold or made with a toasted hoagie. Roll then put in the oven to heat the meat and melt the cheeses (I give the directions for serving hot after the directions for serving cold). Lettuce and sauerkraut? Why not! To make this hoagie with the meat cold, toast the hoagie then put lettuce on bottom of each roll and then add 2 tomato slices to each. Follow with 3 salami on each and then cut provolone cheese in 1/2. Put 2 halves on each roll then 3 slices of ham folded in half. Then cut the mozzarella cheese in 1/2 and put 2 halves on each. Add 3 slices of cappacola ham (spicy Italian ham) then divide the very thinly sliced red onion between both rolls. Cut the stems off the pepperoninis. Remove the membranes and seeds. Place 3 on each roll and add the sauerkraut relish. Place 2 sandwich picks in each one. Cut each in half. Place in the center of two large dinner plates or in sandwich baskets. These sandwiches are so big and complete; all I would serve with them is a good kosher pickle. To serve this sandwich hot, first toast the hoagie so it stays crunchy. Leave off lettuce and tomatoes. Layer all the meats and cheeses with the onion and pepperoninis. Place in a 400-degree oven. Check after 5 min. If not hot and bubbly, let it go another 3 to 4 min. Be careful not to let it burn. Remove from oven place on flat surface and add lettuce, tomatoes, and sauerkraut relish. Place 2 sandwich picks in each, cut and serve. If you want to prepare the meat and cheeses the day before, layer them as I have instructed. Put in a sealable plastic bag or wrap in plastic, but do not do this anymore than one day ahead; the cheese will get wet. You can also layer the meats and cheeses separately. They do not have to alternate. The reason I cut the cheeses in half is because they will hang off the roll, and you will lose a lot of it. The ham is folded so it fits better, not hanging off the roll. I am not a neat sandwich freak; I just think they look more appetizing with everything is not hanging off the roll or bread. Stack it high—a mile high! To make this sandwich into a salad, cut up the iceberg lettuce, put it in a mixing bowl, add the sauerkraut relish cut up all the meats and cheeses into bite-size pieces, cut the pepperoninis into rings, and dice or slice the red onion. Then toss it all together. Either serve it in a large serving bowl buffet style on large dinner plates or small salad plates. The hoagie rolls can be toasted served on the side.

Sauerkraut Relish

This relish can be made with store bought sauerkraut or you can make your own. I will give the recipe for making your own sauerkraut following this recipe.

2 c. sauerkraut
1/2 c. carrots
1 c. celery
1/2 c. white onion
1 c. green bell peppers
1/4 c. sugar
1/4 c. cider vinegar
1 t. caraway seeds

You will need a food processor or blender for this relish. Peel the carrots, cut them into small pieces, cut the celery into pieces about 1 in. long so it does not string, peel, cut onion into small pieces, and cut the bell pepper in 1/2. Then remove the stem, membrane, and seeds. Cut into small pieces and put all this in a food processor or blender. Add the sugar, vinegar, and caraway seeds. Blend until the consistency of pickle relish. This relish will keep for a long time in the fridge. You will find many uses for it such as burgers, brats, hot dogs, or even a Rueben sandwich.

Sauerkraut

6 c. green head cabbage
2 T. ks
2 c. vinegar (cider or red wine)

Thin slice the cabbage or buy already shredded. Heat up a large skillet; you will need room to stir the sauerkraut. Put in the cabbage. Add salt. Stir and cook until the cabbage starts to cook. Keep stirring on medium heat. Once the cabbage starts to really cook, slowly add the vinegar. Be careful not to breathe in too hard; the vapor will choke you. I know; I have done that. Cook the sauerkraut until the vinegar is evaporated and the kraut is done. Make sure you keep this in the fridge until used; it will last several weeks. Enjoy.

Daniel Portobello Club with Jalapeno Pickled Vegetables

The jalapeno pickled vegetables can be made fresh, or you may find a variety at the store. Fresh or pickled jalapenos can be used. For this recipe I will use the bought, pickled jalapenos. This does need to set in the fridge for at least a week before being used. Now that I have your curiosity going, I will give you the recipe for jalapeno-pickled vegetables before the sandwich. This recipe will make more than what you need for this sandwich, but it will last months in the fridge, and you will find lots of uses for it. Remember, vinegar is your best preservative.

Jalapeno Pickled Vegetables

Use equal amounts of everything, making sure it is well covered with the vinegar when you put it in the fridge.

pickled jalapenos
carrots
zucchini
baby corn
red onion
cauliflower
cider vinegar

cayenne pepper
small amount of ks
fgbp. or peppercorns

In a container with a tight-fitting lid, use whole or sliced pickled jalapenos. Peel or do not peel the carrots; the choice is yours. Slice it very thin. Add to jalapenos. Slice the zucchini very thin. Add to the jalapenos. Take the baby corn. Cut each ear in 1/2 the long way and add to the jalapeno mix. Slice the red onion very thin or dice. Add to the pool. The cauliflower, cut into flowerets then slice very thin. Add to the rest. Toss in some salt and pepper or peppercorns. Mix well. Mix the cayenne pepper with the vinegar. Pour enough over the jalapeno mix to cover. Seal with a lid that seals well and tight. Put in the back of the fridge; do not open it for one week. Enjoy. This jalapeno mix can also be chopped well together to make a relish.

Portobello Club

2 ea. Large portobello mushrooms
2 c. Romaine lettuce shredded
4 ea. Slices of tomato
2 c. Water cress (optional)
2 ea. Slices smoked mozzarella cheese
2 ea. Slices Monterey jack cheese
6 ea. Slices of dark rye bread
1 c. Jalapeno pickled vegetables
8 ea. Sandwich picks

I do not put a lot of vegetables on this sandwich because there are a lot of them in the jalapeno pickled vegetables. I start this sandwich by firing up the grill to cook the Portobello mushrooms. If you do not have a grill or do not want to bother with it, use a skillet or the oven. Clean the gills out of the underside of the Portobello mushroom. To do this I use a spoon just carefully scrape them away. I do this because they do not taste very good. Coat the mushrooms with evoo. Add salt and pepper. Place on the hot grill or on a cookie sheet in a 400-degree oven. It should only take about 10 min. to cook the mushrooms. You want them soft and moist, not dry and wrinkly. I prefer to cook them top-side down no matter how I cook them. Toast the bread either in the oven while mushrooms are cooking or in a toaster. Place 4 slices of the toast on a flat surface. Thin slice the romaine lettuce. Divide between the 4 slices of bread. Place 2 slices of tomatoes on 2 slices of toast. The water cress is optional; it just adds another level of crunch. Divide it between the 4 slices of toast and place the smoked mozzarella cheese on 2 slices. Place the Monterey Jack cheese slices on the other 2. When the Portobello mushrooms are done cooking, place them on 2 slices of the toast. On the other 2 slices place the drained jalapeno pickled vegetables. Stack the slices of toasted rye with the Portobello mushrooms on top of the toasted rye, with the jalapeno pickled vegetables on top, and the last 2 slices of toasted rye bread on top. Put in 2 sandwich picks. Either cut in half to serve on large dinner plates or place 4 sandwich picks into the sandwich at 12, 3, 6, and 9; that is according to the clock. Cut with a knife diagonally between the picks so you have 4 pieces of each sandwich. Lay on the large dinner plates on their side with cut sides facing up. They look really neat that way. I suggest serving some really good quality potato chips with this sandwich to help with the heat of the jalapeno-pickled vegetables. Yes, this is another sandwich that can be served as a salad. Toast the rye bread for croutons. To do this, cut into bite size pieces, toss with evoo, granulated garlic, granulated onion, and dried Italian seasoning. Toast in a preheated 350 degree oven. It only takes maybe 10 minutes at the most; I would bake for 5 minutes, stir, and return to the oven for no more than 5 minutes more, remove from oven, and let cook. Store in a closed container until used. This is a great way to use breads and buns that are getting stale. Cut the romaine lettuce into bite-sized pieces. Put in a mixing bowl, cut up everything else, toss with the romaine—even the jalapeno-pickled vegetables—and add some evoo. A flavored bottled from the specialty store would be great; there are some that have heat to them. Either put on large dinner plates, small salad plates, or in a large serving bowl. Add the rye croutons or serve them on the side.

Cassidy Tuna Wasabi Wrap

2 6 oz. Tuna steaks
6 ea. Tomato slices
12 ea. Cucumber slices
2 c. Nappa cabbage
1 c. Red onion
1 c. Sesame wasabi soy sauce (recipe follows)
2 ea. Large flour tortillas
2 c. Pickled ginger cucumber salad (recipe follows)
4 ea. Sandwich picks

There is just something about a grilled tuna steak with fresh tomatoes, cucumbers, red onions, and nappa cabbage. The tuna steaks will be best if marinated in some of the sesame wasabi soy sauce for 4 to 6 hours before grilling or searing in a skillet. Of course tuna is best when eaten rare. If rare is not your taste, by all means cook the tuna to your liking. Slice the tomatoes very thin; thick-sliced tomatoes do not wrap well since they are too bulky. They can also be diced, which is the same with the cucumbers. I like to leave the skin on but peel it if you like. They can be cut in half (and the seeds can be removed) then sliced thin. The nappa cabbage needs to be sliced very thin as well as the onion, or the onion can be diced. Warm the tortillas. Lay them on a flat surface. Slice the tuna steaks very thin or dice. Place on the tortillas about 2 inches from the bottom of the tortilla. Layer on the tomatoes, cucumbers, cabbage, and onion. Drizzle with the sesame wasabi soy sauce. Fold the bottom of the tortilla up over the tuna fold in the sides. Roll up the tortilla. Add 2 sandwich picks to each roll up (if you are going to sear the roll up, add picks after). This also can be seared on a griddle or skillet with a small amount of oil. Sear on all sides. Cut in half. Place on large dinner plates. Serve with a side of the pickled ginger cucumber salad. To make this a salad, cut up the nappa cabbage. Place on 2 large salad bowls. The tomatoes can be diced or cut into wedges placed around the bowl. Slice or dice the cucumbers and do the same with the red onion. Slice the tuna steaks. Lay across the salad. Drizzle with the sesame wasabi soy sauce. Yes, this sauce can be used like a vinaigrette. Of course, some rice wine vinegar and canola salad or vegetable can be blended with the sesame wasabi soy sauce. Do 1 c. vinegar to 2 c. oil. Add 1/2 c. of the sesame wasabi soy sauce. Blend well.

Sesame Wasabi Soy Sauce

1/2 c. sesame oil
1 T. soy sauce
1 T. wasabi powder or paste
1 t. garlic
1/4 t. ks
1/2 t. fgbp

Put everything together and blend well. If you do not use all this sauce it will keep in the fridge for a long time. After about 3 to 4 days the heat of the wasabi is gone. The flavor is still there, but if you want the kick back just add another 1 t. of wasabi.

Pickled Ginger Cucumber Salad

1/2 c. pickled ginger and juice
2 c. sliced cucumbers
1 c. white onion
1 c. rice wine vinegar
1/2–1 c. sugar
1/2 t. ks
1 t. fgbp

Pickled ginger? What is it, and where do I get it? It is exactly what it says it is—very thin-sliced fresh ginger that has been pickled. If you do home canning it is something you can make yourself. I buy it at the grocery store where the Asian food is sold, in a glass jar. The color is pink. When you go to a Chinese buffet, if they have sushi, they have it in a bowl. This salad only gets better the longer it sits in the fridge. I suggest if the jar of pickled ginger is larger than 1/2 c. just increase the recipe to match the quantity. You will find a lot of uses for this salad. Now let's make the salad. Measure out the pickled ginger into a mixing bowl or storage container with lid to keep it in. If you do not use the entire jar, leave enough juice in the jar to cover what you do not use. Keep the rest in the fridge. You will also find lots of uses for it. The cucumbers can be peeled or unpeeled. Deseed or leave the seeds in. I leave the skin on and seeds in. Slice very thin. Add to pickled ginger in bowl. Peel and cut the onion in half. Slice very thin. Add to the ginger and cucumbers. Add the vinegar, 1/2 c. sugar, and salt and pepper. Mix well. If not sweet enough add the rest of the sugar. Store in the fridge. It should only take 24 hrs. If you have ever made refrigerator pickles this is the same thing; just keep out the pickled ginger. This will keep just like store-bought pickles for a long time; in fact, I have never had pickles go bad as long as I keep them in the fridge.

Making Pickled Ginger

2 lbs. fresh young ginger
2 t. ks.
3 c. rice wine vinegar
2 c. sugar

Wash and peel the ginger. A vegetable peeler or a spoon to scrape the ginger works great. Slice very thin. Place in a mixing bowl. Add salt. Toss then let sit for 1 hour. Dry the ginger slices with a paper towel. Place in a clean, heat-proof container—preferably a jar. Mix the rice wine vinegar with the sugar. Place on the stove. Heat to boil. Pour carefully into the container or jar and let cool. The pickled ginger should turn a light pink. If the ginger is old it may not turn pink. The natural color of ginger is light beige. Put a lid on the container store in the fridge. I would give the ginger about a week before tasting.

Jodi Arugula Club with Herb Aioli

Another club? This one is different. It is on a croissant, not 3 slices of bread. What is an aioli? It is actually a mayonnaise with herbs or spices added to it. The easy way is to use processed mayonnaise. The right way is to make your own mayonnaise.

Arugula Club

2 ea. Large croissants
6 ea. Slices bacon
3 ea. Slices of smoked turkey
3 ea. Slices of smoked ham
4 ea. Slices tomato (green would be nice during summer)
4 ea. Slices muenster cheese
1 c. Alfalfa sprouts
1 c. Arugula
1/2 c. Herb aioli
4 ea. Sandwich picks

Cook the bacon crisp. Use the bacon grease to coat the croissants before toasting either in the oven, on the grill, or in a skillet on the stove. Drain the bacon so it is not greasy. Lay the bottoms of the croissants on a flat surface, spread some of the aioli on the bottom croissant, divide the arugula between the 2 bottoms, and add 2 slices of tomato then the muenster cheese using 2 slices on each croissant. Next add 3 slices of the ham folded in half to each and then divide the alfalfa sprouts between the 2. Add the 3 slices of smoked turkey folded in half. Top with 3 slices of bacon. Spread more aioli on the tops. Place on the stack. Put 2 sandwich picks in each. Cut in half. Place on two large dinner plates. Garnish with bread and butter pickles. A great accompaniment to this salad would be a nice, hot bowl of basil tomato soup. All the ingredients for this salad except the croissants can be cut up, tossed together with the herb aioli, served buffet style with the croissants on the side, or plated with a warm croissant on the side. You can also serve the hot basil tomato soup with the salad.

Herb Aioli

1 c. mayonnaise (fresh made or processed the directions for making mayonnaise is in the recipe for Alicia Curried Chicken)
1 t. basil (fresh or dried)
1 t. oregano (fresh or dried)
1/2 t. garlic (fresh or dried)
1/4 t. ks
1/2 t. fgbp

Combine everything and mix well. If you do not use all this, it will keep in the fridge for 2 weeks covered. Discard after 2 weeks.

Anita Marinated Grilled Chicken with Roasted Melon Relish

Another grilled chicken? Pork can also be used instead of chicken. Whichever you use, chicken or pork this sandwich is different.

Marinated Grilled Chicken Sandwich

2 ea. 6 oz. Chicken breast or boneless pork loin
4 ea. Tomato slices
1 c. Spinach
1 c. Roasted melon relish (recipe follows)
4 ea. Slices of bread your choice
1 c. Cumin marinade (recipe follows)
4 ea. Sandwich picks

I believe that the best idea for a chicken sandwich is to marinade the chicken. This insures a juicy, flavorful chicken breast. I chose cumin for this marinade because it goes so well with melons and fruits in general. Marinade the chicken or pork in the cumin marinade for 4 to 6 hrs. before grilling. Overnight is even better; there is no vinegar or acid in this marinade, so the meat will not break down and be mushy when grilled. Toast the bread in a toaster or oven, lay on a flat surface, top 2 slices with the spinach, add the tomato slices, and then add the grilled chicken or pork top with the roasted melon relish. Place the other 2 slices of toasted bread on top. Put 2 sandwich picks in each. Cut in half. Place on 2 large dinner plates. Serve with the pickle of your choice. I suggest serving a pasta salad with this sandwich. To make this sandwich as a salad cut the melons into larger pieces before roasting. Add the cumin and oil to them. Toss, roast. The size of the onion is up to you. Dice the chicken or pork. Add to the melons, use grape or cherry tomatoes, cut in half or dice salad tomatoes into bite-size pieces. Add the spinach and toss everything together. Serve as a buffet salad or place on large dinner plates. I think green chili cornbread would be great with this salad, especially if it was buttered with cayenne pepper butter. To make cayenne pepper butter, simply soften butter and mix cayenne pepper into it. You will find lots of uses for this butter.

Cumin Marinade

1 T. ground cumin
1 T. onion powder
1 T. garlic powder
1/2 t. ks
1 t. fgbp
1 c. canola, salad or vegetable oil

The reason I use onion and garlic powders for this marinade is because they blend in very well with the oil, so you do not have chunks of garlic and onion on your meat. If you prefer fresh onion and garlic, by all means us them. Put everything together in a mixing bowl and blend well. More of the dry mix can be made and stored in a zip lock bag or container stored in a dry place. Measure out what you need. Mix with the oil. Cayenne pepper or crushed red chili can be added to this for extra kick.

Roasted Melon Relish

2 c. honey dew
2 c. cantaloupe
2 c. watermelon
1/2 c. red onion
1/2 t. ground cumin
2 T. canola, salad or vegetable oil
1/4 t. ks
1/2 t. fgbp
1/4 t. crushed red chilies or cayenne pepper (optional)

Preheat oven to 350 degrees. Peel and dice the melons into large pieces. The directions for peeling fruit are in the recipe for Janie S. Fire Roasted Fruit & Chicken. They will be chopped smaller after roasting. Put in a mixing bowl, peel and dice the red onion. Add to the melons; add the oil, salt, pepper, and chilies or cayenne if desired. Mix to coat well. Spray a baking dish. Put melon mix in it. Place in the oven roast for 5 to 10 min. Check after 5 min. If still hard, cook another

5 min. but no more; the melon will turn to mush. You want the melon to be soft but not mushy. Let cool. This relish can be put in a blender to chop fine or chopped by hand; it depends how fine you want the relish to be. This relish will keep in the fridge for about four days before the melon turns bad. Pineapple can be added.

Wes Roasted Beef Spread Sandwich

That roast you cooked yesterday does not have to be hash tomorrow. If you have a food processor or one of those metal grinders that attach to the counter or table, you are in business. Your family will love this roasted beef spread. By the way, turkey, ham, bologna, or any lunch meat can be used to make this spread.

Roasted Beef Spread

2 c. cooked roast beef (steak can also be used)
1/2 c. mayonnaise (homemade or processed the recipe for making mayonnaise is in the recipe for Alicia Curried Chicken)
1/2 c. sweet pickles
1/2 c. white onion
1/4 t. ks
1/2 t. fgbp

Trim all the fat off the meat, cut into chunks no more than 1 in. Place in food processor. Add pickles, onions, salt, pepper, and mayonnaise. Blend until the consistency you want. Taste for salt, pepper, sweetness of pickles, onion, and mayonnaise and adjust taste. Add more of what you want. If you use a grinder, put the meat in the grinder. As you are grinding the meat add the pickles and onion after grinding. Add the salt, pepper, and mayonnaise. Taste and adjust for flavor.

Roasted Beef Spread Sandwich

Every time I served this at a party I used hamburger buns. It seemed to go very well with them. I served it with bread one time, and every one said, "Where are the burger buns?" There are other buns that are great; I also like those ones called potato rolls or dinner rolls. If you use smaller rolls other than hamburger buns I would recommend using 3 rolls per person.

2 ea. Hamburger buns
4 ea. Sliced tomato
2 ea. Leaves of lettuce
1 c. Roast beef spread
1/4 c. Mayonnaise
2 ea. Sandwich picks

The buns do not need to be toasted for these sandwiches. You can if you would like. Lay the bottoms of the buns on a flat surface. Spread the top and bottoms of the buns with the mayonnaise. Place half of the roast beef spread on each bun bottom. Top with the tomato slices then the lettuce leaves (your choice of lettuce). Place the tops on. Place a sandwich pick in each one. Place on two large dinner plates serve with more sweet pickles on the side. Creamy coleslaw would be great served with this sandwich. Not in my wildest dreams can I come up with a salad for roast beef spread. As an appetizer on crackers or corn chips, yes, but as a salad, no.

Phoenix Turkey, Mango, & Jicama Sandwich

Now you know what to do with that leftover turkey. If the turkey is smoked, that is even better. Yes, this recipe can be made with chicken, also. The sweetness of the mango and crunch plus sweetness of the jicama is just amazing.

Turkey, Mango, & Jicama Salad

2 c. turkey
1 c. mango (fresh or frozen)
1 c. jicama
1/4 c. mayonnaise (fresh made or processed the recipe for making mayonnaise is in the recipe for Alicia Curried Chicken)
1/4 c. green onion
1 t. tarragon (fresh or dried)
1/4 t. ks
1/2 t/ fgbp

Dice the turkey small. Place in a mixing bowl. To prep the mango you can peel first with a vegetable peeler or a paring knife. Cut the mango off the seed. Fine dice and add to turkey; the jicama has a very thin, brown skin that has to be removed. A vegetable peeler or paring knife works great for this, fine dice. Add to turkey. Slice the green onions very thin and add to the rest. Next add the mayonnaise, salt, pepper, and tarragon and mix well. Why tarragon? It goes very well with turkey and mango. If you do not like tarragon, try using basil.

Turkey, Mango, & Jicama Sandwich

I like to serve this on a toasted hoagie roll or a Kaiser roll
2 ea. Hoagie rolls or Kaiser rolls
2 c. Turkey, mango and jicama salad (recipe above)
1 c. Shredded cabbage
1/2 c. Mango mayonnaise (recipe follows)
4 ea. Sandwich picks

I do not use lettuce on this salad. The shredded cabbage works great for sweetness and crunch. Spread butter on the rolls and toast in the oven or in a skillet on the stove. Lay on a flat surface. Spread the mango mayonnaise on both sides of each roll. On the bottom half of both rolls put the cabbage. Then top with half of the turkey, mango, and jicama salad on each one. Place the tops on the rolls. Put in 2 sandwich picks in each. Cut in half. Place on large dinner plates. A bowl of fresh berries, bananas, and nuts would be great as a side for this sandwich. This is another one of those sandwiches that makes a great salad, also. Either place baby greens or spinach on large dinner plates top with the turkey, mango, and jicama salad. Toss everything together and serve on large dinner plates or toss everything together and serve buffet style. Some warm banana nut bread with cinnamon butter would be great served with it.

Mango Mayonnaise

1 c. mayonnaise (homemade or processed the recipe for making mayonnaise is in the recipe for Alicia Curried Chicken)
1/2 c. mango (fresh or frozen)
1/4 t. ks
1/4 t. fgbp

Fine dice the mango. Add to the mayonnaise. Add the salt and pepper. Mix well. You can also blend this together to make it creamy. Green onion can also be added.

Chris L. Open Face Steak & Balsamic Cayenne Pepper Onions Sandwich

I know what you are saying. Finally she added a steak sandwich, not just a steak sandwich. It's a steak sandwich with some flavor and heat. A steak sandwich is not complete, as far as I am concerned, without onions.

Open Face Steak & Balsamic Cayenne Pepper Onions Sandwich

2 ea. 6 oz. Beef steaks grilled (delmonico, rib eye, sirloin or New York your choice)
6 ea. Slices grilled green tomatoes
2 c. Balsamic cayenne pepper onions (recipe follows)
2 c. Arugula or spinach or both
2 ea. Slices Texas toast
4 ea. Slices smoked cheddar cheese
1 1/4 c. Balsamic cayenne pepper marinade (recipe follows)
2 ea. Grilled sliced or wedged potatoes (recipe follows)
1 c. Balsamic cayenne pepper aioli (recipe follows)

To make this great steak sandwich make sure to marinate the steak for at least but not more than 4 to 6 hours before grilling. Cook to your liking; mine is rare. Add the cheese, the move to a cooler spot on the grill and out of the way. You can cook the tomatoes and toast the bread. If you do not like green tomatoes, red will do. I like green; they have a snappy, crisp taste. Put them on the grill after the steaks come off. Right where the steaks were grilling I suggest spraying them with nonstick spray first. Grill until just softened a little no more than a minute or two. The Texas toast can be done at the same time. Spread both sides with butter or oil—your choice. Grill on both sides until well toasted. The reason I grill on both sides is because this helps the toast stay crunchy longer. Lay the bread on a flat surface top with the steaks. Add the balsamic cayenne pepper onions then the grilled tomatoes. Top with the arugula or spinach or both. Cut in 1/2 or leave whole. Place on two large dinner plates. Balsamic vinegar can be drizzled over the top. A side I like to make to serve with this steak sandwich is grilled potatoes. The best potatoes to use for this are leftover bakers. Of course the potatoes can be baked that day then either cut in slices about 3/4 in. to 1 in. thick or wedged. Dip them in either butter or evoo. Put on the grill with the steaks. A balsamic cayenne pepper aioli can be served with them.

Balsamic Cayenne Pepper Marinade

1/4 c. balsamic vinegar (traditional or chili infused)
2 t. cayenne pepper
1 c. evoo (plain or chili infused)
1/4 t. ks
1 t. fgbp

Add everything together in a bowl and mix well. Completely coat both sides of the steaks. Place in a dish. Pour on the rest of the marinade cover refrigerate until ready to use. Remove from the fridge after about 30 min. before you're ready to grill to remove some of the chill. Discard the marinade after using. A large quantity of the marinade can be mixed and stored in the fridge, removing only what you need. Sometimes the evoo sets up like grease. This is not a bad thing; just let it sit out for about 30 minutes. Stir well; it is ready to use. This marinade is also great for chicken, pork, seafood, or fish. It is also great for grilling vegetables.

Balsamic Cayenne Pepper Onions

6 c. sliced onions (white or red)
1/4. evoo (plain or chili infused)
1 c. balsamic vinegar (traditional or chili infused)
2 t. cayenne pepper
1/4 t. ks
1/2 t. fgbp

Vidalia onions are great for this dish or any sweet, white, or red onion. Slice the onions about 1/2 thick. Heat a skillet on medium heat until hot. Carefully add the evoo then carefully add the onions. Stir constantly to prevent burning. When the onions have cooked well and are very soft with a clear color, carefully add the other ingredients. Cook until all the moisture is gone, stirring often to prevent burning. If you want to cook a lot more they will keep in the fridge for about a week and are great for almost any dish.

Grilled, Sliced, or Wedged Potatoes

2 ea. baked or boiled potatoes with skin on
1/4 c. evoo (plain or chili infused) or melted butter
ks. to taste
fgbp. to taste

This is a great way to use leftover baked or boiled potatoes. I prefer to leave the skin on; it holds them together. Slice the potatoes about 3/4 in. thick or cut in wedges the length of the potatoes. Dip in the evoo or butter. Place carefully on the grill. The evoo or butter will cause flaming for just a quick time. If you do not want this, use pan spray instead of the evoo or butter, turning as desired. Grill to your taste. Sprinkle with the salt and pepper after removing from the grill.

Balsamic Cayenne Pepper Aioli

1 c. mayonnaise (homemade or purchased; the recipe
for making your own mayonnaise is in the recipe for
Alicia Curried Chicken)
2 to 4 T. balsamic vinegar (traditional or chili infused)
1 to 2 t. cayenne pepper
1/4 t. ks
1/2 t. fgbp

Put the mayonnaise in a mixing bowl. Add 2 T.
balsamic vinegar, 1 t. cayenne pepper, ks, and fgbp. Mix
well. Taste and add more balsamic. If you want more
balsamic, taste, and add more cayenne pepper if desired.
This aioli makes a great spread for other sandwiches
and a great dip for grilled or roasted vegetables as well
as raw vegetables. I am sure you will have no trouble
finding uses for it. This will keep for two weeks only in
the fridge. Discard after that time. The flavor does get
better after a few days.